The
SOUTHERN BAKING COOKBOOK

60 Comforting Recipes Full of *Down-South Flavor*

JENN DAVIS

Founder of the blog Two Cups Flour

PAGE STREET
PUBLISHING CO.

PAGE STREET
PUBLISHING CO.

First published in 2021 by

Page Street Publishing Co.

27 Congress Street, Suite 105

Salem, MA 01970

www.pagestreetpublishing.com

Distributed by Macmillan, sales in Canada by The Canadian Manda Group.

25 24 23 22 21   1 2 3 4 5

ISBN-13: 978-1-64567-346-0

ISBN-10: 1-64567-346-4

Library of Congress Control Number: 2021931265

Cover and book design by Rosie Stewart for Page Street Publishing Co.

Photography by Jennifer Davis

Printed and bound in China

Table of Contents

Introduction

My love for baking evolved organically. I have gone from mixing cookie dough while standing on a small stool as a child, to testing cake recipes with friends in college, to writing a baking blog. The path that led me here saw me hopping along the stepping-stones of drawing, animal medicine, and horse training before I finally landed on food photography. I may have arrived at my current station via a different route than many, but a passion for the culinary world was always there.

My fondest memories always involve food in some fashion. There's something about a smell or taste that can instantly trigger a feeling. Maybe it's the scent of warm bread filling the house that makes you feel all cozy. Or the first bite into a ripe yellow peach that lets you know summer is finally here. Then there are the delights accompanying cold-weather holidays: pecan pie, hot chocolate, buttermilk pancakes smothered in maple syrup on a lazy weekend morning. Every recipe has its own story, and I bet you have a few that make you think of a place, person, or occasion with a smile—same as me.

I grew up in a family that loves good cuisine. Whether we're growing it ourselves, sharing a family recipe, styling a table, or creating a special dessert, it's always done with thoughtful consideration.

Growing up in the South—North Carolina to be exact—I was taught early on that anything made from scratch is always the best. My father taught me how to grow vegetables, when to harvest seasonal fruit, and how to connect with farmers. From local dairy milk, to grape orchards, and back to homegrown tomatoes, I received my education at the source of the product, not the checkout line. The information passed down to me was priceless, as it came not just from my father but a horticulturist.

When I eat blueberries, I think of walking in my rubber boots along a path lined with meandering vines on a cold, foggy morning, filling my basket and sneaking the occasional handful of berries into my mouth. I never pour a glass of milk without thinking of milking Holsteins. There's not a tomato picked that doesn't make me think of white-bread tomato sandwiches. From picking apples in the Appalachian Mountains to gathering muscadines near the coast, my life has always been surrounded by the bounty of nature.

Today, the best part is using all these wonderful ingredients in a recipe and sharing it with others. This is where the magic happens! My mother, an avid home baker and artist, instilled in me her love of preparing and presenting food. No store-bought birthday cakes or frozen pies made their way into her kitchen.

Elaborately decorated desserts, perfectly wrapped bundles of fudge, precisely frosted cookies, and fluffy breads have always been her version of the perfect gift. Whether it was a simple request, party, or holiday, each baked good was displayed on a proper dish with purposeful toppings. This is how I first came to appreciate that food is more than mere sustenance—it is art, passion, therapy, and, above all, love.

I didn't know it then, but as a child I was already under a huge foodie influence. All I knew at the time was that I had a serious sweet tooth, and playing with food in the kitchen was a delicious way to soothe it.

As you may already know, I'm a full-flavor, sugar, real-butter, buttermilk, fresh-fruit, and dark-chocolate kinda girl. The recipes in this book are my interpretations and beloved versions of southern baking classics using the ingredients I grew up with. Now, let's put on our aprons, grab some measuring cups, and preheat that oven!

Jenn

Good Ole Pies and Cobblers

If you asked for my most-loved recipe to make or eat, it would always be pie! I just can't get enough of that homemade flaky, buttery crust. Whether it's tangy citrus, rich chocolate, or savory vegetable, I'm all about the homemade pie. When southern baking comes to mind, I always envision a summer fruit pastry cooling in an open window, hot cobblers with melting ice cream, or fried hand pies wrapped with a linen. The memories of my grandmother asking me if I want a thick or thin slice of pumpkin pie on Thanksgiving, laughing and pitting cherries with red-stained hands, and snuggling up with a huge serving of chicken pot pie on a snowy evening are the ones I truly cherish. This chapter is an array of seasonal recipes that evoke a bit of nostalgia.

TIPS FOR SUCCESS

- There's no such thing as a bad pie; just use fresh ingredients and enjoy the process.
- Keep your butter cold and hands floured, and chill your crusts before baking them. If you have cracks in your unbaked crust, try to patch them and avoid rerolling the dough. Overworking the dough will make it tough.
- Place pie pans on rimmed baking sheets in the oven to catch any fillings that may bubble over.
- Hot pies need some time to cool in order for their fillings to set.
- Store your pies in airtight containers in the fridge.
- I love using metal pie pans because they ensure a great bake on the crust without a soggy bottom.

HOMEMADE PIE CRUST

YIELDS

2 (9" [23-cm]) pie crusts or
1 (9" [23-cm]) pie crust with a
decorative edge

1 cup (227 g) unsalted butter

2½ cups (313 g) all-purpose flour,
plus more as needed

1 tbsp (13 g) sugar

1 tsp kosher salt

1 tsp ground cinnamon or ground
ginger (optional)

1 large egg, cold and lightly beaten

1 tbsp (15 ml) apple cider vinegar

4 to 5 tbsp (60 to 75 ml) ice water,
divided, plus more if needed

Flaky, buttery homemade pie crust is one recipe you need in your baking back pocket. I find the whole process of making pie dough therapeutic. Not to mention, the flavor of an all-butter pie crust is truly mouthwatering. This is my favorite version and the one I use for all my pies and fruit galettes. It's a simple mixture that takes almost no time to bring together. Once you taste a homemade crust, you'll never bake a pie without it. I like to add a teaspoon of cinnamon or ginger to the dough for a little more flavor. Make the crust ahead and keep it in the fridge or freezer so you'll be ready when a pie calls your name!

Note: My best tips for making a great pie crust are to keep all of the ingredients cold and to not overwork the dough.

Grate your butter or cut it into small cubes. Place it in the freezer to chill for about 5 minutes. The grated butter helps create a flakier crust and the warmth of your hands will help it mix into the flour.

In a large bowl, whisk together the flour, sugar, salt, and cinnamon (if using). Add the chilled butter. If you grated the butter, work it into the flour with your hands until the mixture resembles coarse cornmeal. If you cut the butter into cubes, use a pastry cutter to work it into the flour initially, and then use your hands. Small pebbles of butter left in the mixture is fine. I love seeing small butter splotches in my pie dough!

Pour in the egg and stir the mixture with a wooden spoon. The egg helps make the dough more pliable and easier to roll out. Next, add the vinegar and 3 tablespoons (45 ml) of the ice water. The vinegar also helps tenderize the dough, but it will not alter the flavor. As you slowly bring the ingredients together with your hands, add the remaining 1 to 2 tablespoons (15 to 30 ml) of ice water 1 tablespoon (15 ml) at a time. If you are making the pie crust during cool weather, you may not use all the water indicated in the recipe. If you are making the crust during hot weather, sometimes you may need an extra 1 tablespoon (15 ml). I like to add the water slowly and judge the texture of the dough as it comes together.

As you spoon in the cold water, start packing the mixture into a dough ball with your hands. The dough's texture should be slightly tacky but not wet or sticky. If it is still crumbly and not packing together, add a little more ice water.

Once your dough has formed, weigh and divide it into two equal pieces. Knead each half gently into a disk shape, which will make it easier to roll out.

Wrap each disk with plastic wrap and refrigerate the dough for 1 hour to allow it to chill and rest. If you're not planning to use the dough right away, it can stay in the fridge for 3 days. To freeze the dough, wrap it well in heavy-duty, freezer-safe aluminum foil or a freezer-safe bag. Pie dough can be frozen for 6 months and should be brought to nearly room temperature before you roll it out. Dough that is ready to roll out should indent slightly when you push down on it with your finger.

Lightly dust a work surface with flour. Lightly dust a rolling pin and your hands as well. Place the chilled dough on the prepared work surface. Place the rolling pin in the center of the disk and roll it away from yourself and then back toward yourself. Rotate the dough and repeat this rolling method, moving outward from the center of the dough, for an even layer.

Follow the desired recipe directions from this point.

NOTE

This recipe works beautifully for making hand pies, like my Mini Strawberry-Lime Pies (page 21) and Thanksgiving Hand Pies (page 38).

HERB AND CHEESE GALETTE CRUST

YIELDS

1 (10 to 12" [25- to 30-cm]) galette crust

2½ cups (313 g) all-purpose flour, plus more as needed

1 tsp sugar

1 tsp kosher salt

1½ tbsp (6 g) minced fresh thyme

1 cup (227 g) unsalted butter, cold and cut into small cubes

1 large egg, lightly beaten

¼ cup (21 g) grated hoop or extra sharp Cheddar cheese

4 tbsp (60 ml) ice water, plus more if needed

We all love fruit and sweet pies, but don't forget about savory pies! Adding a touch of cheese and herbs to an all-butter pie crust instantly transforms the flavor profile for meat and veggie pies. You can substitute any herb or grated firm cheese you prefer. Get a little sassy with a sprinkle of flaky salt mixed with small seeds on the outer crust for some crunch. This is my trusted crust recipe for chicken pie, quiches, and tomato galettes that I know you'll love.

The steps to make the savory dough are similar to the steps for my Homemade Pie Crust (page 10): In a large bowl, whisk together the flour, sugar, salt, and thyme. Drop in the cold butter cubes and work them into the flour with a pastry cutter or your fingertips until the mixture resembles coarse cornmeal.

Add the egg and stir it into the dough with a wooden spoon. Mix in the hoop cheese until it is evenly dispersed. Next, add the water 1 tablespoon (15 ml) at a time. If you are making the crust during cool weather, you may not use all the water indicated in the recipe. If it's hot outside, you may need an extra tablespoon (15 ml). I like to add the water slowly and judge the texture of the dough as it comes together. As you spoon in the cold water, start packing the mixture into a dough ball with your free hand. The dough's texture should be slightly tacky but not wet or sticky. If it's still crumbly and not packing together, add a little more water.

Once your dough is formed, flatten it into a disk shape so that it's easier to roll out. Cover the dough with plastic wrap and refrigerate it for 1 hour to allow it to chill and rest. If you're not planning to use the dough right away, it can stay in the fridge for up to 3 days. To freeze the dough, wrap it well in heavy-duty, freezer-safe aluminum foil, or place it in a freezer-safe bag. Store the wrapped dough in an airtight container in the freezer. Pie dough can be frozen for 6 months and then brought nearly to room temperature before rolling it out.

Place the chilled dough on a lightly floured surface. Lightly dust your rolling pin and hands with flour. Place the rolling pin in the center of the disk and roll it away from yourself and then back toward yourself. Rotate the dough and repeat this rolling method, moving outwardly from the center of the dough to create an even layer.

Follow the desired recipe directions from this point.

PEACH AND PLUM SLAB PIE

CRUST

1 recipe Homemade Pie Crust
(page 10)

½ recipe Homemade Pie Crust
(optional; page 10)

Sparkling sugar, as needed

FILLING

¼ cup (55 g) light brown sugar,
packed

¼ cup (50 g) granulated sugar

¼ cup (31 g) all-purpose flour, plus
more as needed

2 tbsp (16 g) cornstarch

½ tsp ground cinnamon

½ tsp ground nutmeg

¼ tsp fine sea salt

1 tbsp (15 ml) sourwood honey

½ tsp orange blossom water

¼ tsp pure almond extract

1 tsp pure vanilla extract

2 tbsp (30 ml) peach brandy
(optional)

2 cups (308 g) ½" (13-mm)-thick
slices peeled fresh yellow peaches

2 cups (308 g) ½" (13-mm)-thick
slices fresh red plums

EGG WASH

1 large egg

1 tsp water

Peach pie is hands down my ideal southern dessert. Hot or cold, plain or with ice cream—I just can't get enough of homemade pastry and yellow peaches. For years I have picked fresh peaches from the local orchards to make lattice pies. But recently I added a few red plums to the filling for a flavor swirl of sweetness and tartness. Then I mixed in a bit of peach brandy for a hint of western Carolina flavor. A splash of booze is totally optional, but if you live anywhere near Appalachia, homemade peach brandy is everywhere and goes great with ice cream. So why not add it to a hot fruit pie, right? This recipe makes about as much dessert as two 9-inch (23-cm) pies, so be sure to invite some friends over to help you eat it all.

Before we get started, I want to point out that making a fruit pie requires several rounds of chilling the dough and filling in the fridge. It's important to keep pie dough cold to prevent it from tearing. First, you will make the pie crust dough, then the fruit filling. Assembly will require making the bottom crust, chilling it, adding the fruit and top crust, chilling the entire pie, adding the decoration (if using), and chilling the pie a final time before baking it. Be sure to read through the following steps before beginning this recipe and to chill that pie before it goes into the hot oven.

To make the crust, use the full recipe of Homemade Pie Crust to make the bottom and top layers of your slab pie. Weigh and divide the dough into two disks and place them in the fridge. If you would like to make the optional decorative outer braid, you will also need to make the ½ recipe of Homemade Pie Crust—keep in mind that you can still make the slab pie without the decorative braid. Chill the full recipe of Homemade Pie Crust and the ½ recipe of Homemade Pie Crust (if using) according to the instructions on page 11.

Set out a 9 x 13–inch (23 x 33–cm) nonstick baking sheet that has a ½- to ¾-inch (1.3- to 1.9-cm) rim. You don't need to spray the baking sheet, but if it's nonstick, a light coating of butter will help.

While the dough is in the fridge, prepare the filling. In a medium bowl, whisk together the brown sugar, granulated sugar, flour, cornstarch, cinnamon, nutmeg, and salt. Add the honey, orange blossom water, almond extract, vanilla extract, and brandy (if using) to the sugar mixture. Mix everything to combine.

Place the sliced peaches and plums in a large bowl. Pour the sugar mixture over the fruit. Using your hands or a soft rubber spatula, gently fold the fruit and sugar mixture together to evenly coat the fruit. Lightly cover the filling with a tea towel and place the bowl in the fridge while you roll out the dough.

(CONTINUED)

PEACH AND PLUM SLAB PIE (CONTINUED)

Lightly dust a work surface with flour. Place one of the dough disks from the full recipe of Homemade Pie Crust on the work surface, and roll it out into a rectangle that is roughly 11 x 15 inches (28 x 38 cm) —slightly larger than the baking sheet. Carefully lower the dough into the baking sheet and fit it to the corners by pressing in gently with your fingertips. Tuck any overhanging crust underneath itself and softly press it against the lip of the baking sheet. Place the dough-lined baking sheet in the fridge to chill for about 15 minutes.

To make the egg wash, use a fork to beat together the egg and water in a small bowl. Set the egg wash aside.

Roll out the second disk of dough from the full recipe of Homemade Pie Crust into a rectangle that is roughly 10 x 13 inches (25 x 33 cm)—almost the same size as your baking sheet. Remove the dough-lined baking sheet and fruit filling from the fridge. Spoon the filling into the cold bottom crust and gently level out the slices of fruit to form an even layer. Brush the rim of the bottom crust with the egg wash or cold water to help seal the top and bottom crusts together. Carefully lift the second layer of dough from the work surface and set it on top of the filling. Seal the top and bottom crusts together with your fingertips. With a sharp knife, cut small vents across the top crust in a fun pattern.

Carefully place the slab pie back in the fridge while you make the outer braids (if using). If you do not want to make the outer braids, chill the slab pie for at least 20 minutes, then skip to the next step. Roll out the dough from the ½ recipe of Homemade Pie Crust until it is ⅛ to ¼ inch (3 to 6 mm) thick. Cut it into long, even strips about ⅛ inch (3 mm) thick. French-braid three strips together at a time and set the braided strips aside.

Remove the pie from the fridge, and brush a thin coating of the egg wash across the entire top crust. Place the braids on the rim of the pie, connecting them together and adhering them to the top crust with egg wash where needed. Brush a thin coating of egg wash onto the braids and sprinkle the sparkling sugar over the entire pie crust.

Now it's time for the final chilling step, which is super important to help the dough maintain its shape while it bakes. Set the pie back in the fridge for 20 minutes, allowing the dough to chill and become firm while you preheat the oven.

To bake your slab pie masterpiece, preheat the oven to 425°F (220°C). If you would like to prevent any fruit juice drippings in your oven, line a rimmed baking sheet that is larger than the pie with parchment paper. Carefully place the pie on the prepared baking sheet. Bake the slab pie on the oven's lowest rack for 20 minutes to ensure even browning on the bottom crust. Reduce the oven's temperature to 350°F (180°C) and bake the pie for 35 to 40 minutes. The egg wash creates a shiny golden crust, but if you feel it's getting too brown, loosely cover the pie with tented aluminum foil after 30 minutes. The pie is done when the filling is bubbling through the vents of the golden top crust.

Transfer the slab pie to a wire rack. Let it cool for about 3 hours in order for the filling to set. If you cut the pie while it's still hot, the filling will be runny. Once the pie has cooled, slice that bad boy into servings. If you want to warm the slices, you can put them in the oven at 350°F for 10 minutes, then top them with vanilla ice cream.

SUNSHINE PIE

YIELDS

8 to 10 servings

CRUST

1 (9" [23-cm]) Homemade Pie Crust
(page 10)

EGG WASH

1 large egg

1 tsp water

FILLING

1⅔ cups (332 g) sugar

2 tbsp (12 g) fresh lemon zest

4 tbsp (32 g) all-purpose flour, plus
more as needed

1 cup (240 ml) full-fat buttermilk,
well shaken

½ cup (114 g) unsalted butter,
melted and cooled

2 large eggs, lightly beaten

1 tsp pure vanilla extract

½ tsp pure lemon extract

1¼ packed cups (105 g) sweetened
shredded coconut

Passed to my mother from her father, this has always been a treasured dessert: a marriage between coconut and lemon chess pie resulting in a delicious family recipe known as Sunshine Pie. A yellow circle bursting with coconut and citrus notes that is perfect all by itself, it's probably the easiest pie to make and the fastest to disappear. This is my preferred version, and I know it will bring a smile to your face just like the summer sunshine!

To make Sunshine Pie, you will first need to make the pie crust. Be sure your Homemade Pie Crust dough has chilled and is ready to go. Position the oven rack to the lower third of the oven. Preheat the oven to 425°F (220°C).

Lightly dust a work surface with flour. Set a 9-inch (23-cm) nonstick metal pie pan within arm's reach of the prepared work surface. Roll out the dough on the prepared work surface until it is ⅛ inch (3 mm) thick and about 13 inches (33 cm) in diameter. Lift the dough and lower it into the pie pan. Gently press the dough into the pie pan with the pads of your fingertips. Gently tuck any overhanging dough under itself and crimp the edges. Use a fork to prick the bottom and sides of the crust that touch the pan several times.

Make the egg wash: In a small bowl, use a fork to beat together the egg and water. Lightly coat the egg wash onto the crimped edges of the crust with a pastry brush. Place the pie crust in the freezer for 30 minutes to allow the dough to chill and become firm. Remember, we like a super cold pie crust to go into the oven.

Remove the pie crust from the freezer. Line the crust with parchment paper, making sure the paper hangs over the sides. Fill the pie with pie weights or uncooked beans all the way to the crimped edges. Bake the pie crust for 15 to 17 minutes, until the edges are light golden brown. Carefully remove the pie crust from the oven and, wearing oven mitts, lift the parchment paper with the hot pie weights from the pie crust. Return the pie crust to the oven and bake it for 4 minutes, then take the pie crust out and set it aside to cool. Reduce the oven's temperature to 350°F (180°C). Reposition the oven's rack to the middle third of the oven. Line a medium baking sheet with parchment paper.

Make the filling: In a large bowl, whisk together the sugar, zest, and flour. Pour in the buttermilk, butter, eggs, vanilla, and lemon extract. Stir until all the ingredients are just combined. Fold in the coconut with a rubber spatula to evenly distribute it throughout the filling. You may need to scrape the sides and the bottom of the bowl to make sure everything is incorporated. Pour the filling into the pie crust. Transfer the pie to the prepared baking sheet. Bake the pie for 60 to 65 minutes, until the edges of the pie are golden and there is a light golden hue to the coconut. I like to loosely cover the pie with tented aluminum foil at the 40-minute mark to prevent the coconut from overbrowning. Carefully transfer the pie pan to a wire rack, and let the pie cool for about 2 hours, until it has cooled to room temperature. Then place the pie in the fridge to chill for a minimum of 1 hour. Get ready to enjoy a slice of sweet bliss with a huge mouthful of cold Sunshine Pie!

COZY CHICKEN PIE

YIELDS

8 to 10 servings

CRUST

1 recipe Herb and Cheese Galette Crust (page 12)

FILLING

3 tbsp (42 g) unsalted butter

⅓ cup (42 g) all-purpose flour, plus more as needed

1 cup (240 ml) chicken stock

¾ cup (180 ml) heavy cream

1 tbsp (6 g) finely chopped fresh sage

1 tbsp (6 g) finely chopped fresh thyme

1 tsp sea salt

½ tsp freshly ground black pepper

4 tbsp (60 ml) olive oil, divided

1 cup (52 g) finely chopped yellow onion

1 clove garlic, minced

1 cup (128 g) peeled and thinly sliced carrots

1 cup (150 g) ½" (1.3-cm) green beans

½ cup (50 g) roughly chopped cremini mushrooms

2 cups (280 g) cooked and shredded chicken breast

TOPPING

1½ cups (90 g) panko breadcrumbs

2 tbsp (28 g) unsalted butter, melted

½ tsp dried oregano

½ tsp dried sage

¼ tsp dried thyme

½ tsp paprika

¼ cup (20 g) grated Robusto Gouda cheese

Nothing beats a warm chicken pie fresh from the oven on a cold evening. When I owned a horse farm, after long days of riding and caring for animals, all I wanted to do was stuff myself with a hot meal and fall asleep on the couch. This recipe is the ultimate comfort food to fill a hungry belly and warm a tired body.

Some chicken pies have only top crusts, some are made in casserole dishes with biscuit toppings, and some are made with just a bottom pie crust. I love a good pie crust base to hold all the creamy goodness inside with a flavorful crunchy topping of seasoned panko breadcrumbs mixed with cheese. Not a huge fan of peas and celery, I've adjusted the classic filling to include green beans and mushrooms. It's delicious just baked, but it's even better the next day!

To make Cozy Chicken Pie, you will first need to make the crust. Be sure your Herb and Cheese Galette Crust dough has chilled and is ready to go.

Position the oven rack to the lower third of the oven. Preheat the oven to 425°F (220°C).

Lightly dust a work surface with flour. Set a 9-inch (23-cm) nonstick metal pie pan within arm's reach of the prepared work surface. Roll out the dough on the prepared work surface until it is ⅛ inch (3 mm) thick and about 13 inches (33 cm) in diameter. Lift the dough and lower it into the pie pan. Gently press the dough into the pie pan with the pads of your fingertips. Gently tuck any overhanging dough under itself and crimp the edges. Use a fork to prick the bottom and sides of the crust that touch the pan several times.

Place the pie crust in the freezer for 30 minutes to allow the dough to chill and become firm. Remember, we like a super cold pie crust to go into the oven.

Remove the pie crust from the freezer. Line the crust with parchment paper, making sure the paper hangs over the sides. Fill the pie with pie weights or uncooked beans all the way to the crimped edges. Bake the pie crust for 15 to 17 minutes, until the edges are light golden brown. Carefully remove the pie crust from the oven and, wearing oven mitts, lift the parchment paper with the hot pie weights from the pie crust. Return the pie crust to the oven and bake it for 4 minutes.

Reduce the oven's temperature to 375°F (190°C). Reposition the oven's rack to the middle third of the oven. Line a medium baking sheet with parchment paper.

(CONTINUED)

COZY CHICKEN PIE (CONTINUED)

Next, make the filling. Set a medium saucepan over medium heat and melt the butter. Sprinkle the flour over the melted butter and whisk them together to form a paste. Reduce the heat to low, then pour in the chicken stock and heavy cream, stirring continuously to form a thick gravy. Remove the cream sauce from the heat and transfer it to a large bowl. Stir in the sage, thyme, salt, and black pepper. Cover the bowl with a linen towel and set it aside.

The vegetables need to be slightly cooked before being baked in the pie, or they will be too crunchy. Heat 1 tablespoon (15 ml) of the oil in a medium skillet over medium heat. Add the onion. Sauté the onion for 2 to 3 minutes, until it becomes soft and translucent. Add the remaining 3 tablespoons (45 ml) of oil. Add the garlic, carrots, and green beans to the skillet and cook the mixture for about 2 minutes. Add the mushrooms and cook the mixture for 3 minutes.

Remove the vegetables from the heat and transfer them to the cream sauce. Stir the filling with a rubber spatula to distribute the vegetables evenly throughout the sauce. Add the chicken and mix the ingredients again. Let the filling cool for about 5 minutes while you prepare the topping.

To make the topping, place the breadcrumbs, butter, oregano, sage, thyme, and paprika in a small bowl. Stir the ingredients with a fork to combine them, and then mix in the Robusto Gouda cheese.

Remove the chilled crust from the refrigerator. Transfer the filling to the crust and level out the filling with a spatula. Generously cover the filling with the topping.

Place the pie pan on the prepared baking sheet to catch any filling that bubbles over. Set the pie in the center of the oven's middle rack. Bake the pie for 40 to 45 minutes, until the filling is bubbling and the edges of the crust are golden brown. The breadcrumb topping should be a rich golden brown. If you feel that the breadcrumbs are getting too dark, place a tented sheet of aluminum foil over the pie for the last 10 minutes of baking.

Remove the pie from the oven and place it on a wire rack. Let the pie cool for 10 to 15 minutes. Serve it hot for a delicious comfort-food dinner.

MINI STRAWBERRY-LIME PIES

YIELDS

7 (5" [13-cm]) hand pies

CRUST

1 recipe Homemade Pie Crust
(page 10)

FILLING

2 cups (332 g) fresh strawberries,
tops removed and roughly chopped

1 cup (200 g) sugar

1 tbsp (6 g) fresh lime zest

3 tbsp (45 ml) fresh lime juice

2 tsp (10 ml) pure vanilla extract

2 tbsp (16 g) cornstarch

1 tbsp (8 g) all-purpose flour, plus
more as needed

GINGER SUGAR

2 cups (400 g) sugar

2 tsp (4 g) ground ginger

FOR FRYING

Vegetable oil, as needed

Fried fruit pies coated in sugar are one of the best summer treats. Biting into buttery pastry and having warm fruit ooze across your taste buds is pure bliss. Seasonal fair and festival vendors always have warm, sweet, fried dough ready to serve. Growing up, I showed dairy cows at the North Carolina State Fair, and of all the food I ate, fried dessert reigned supreme. You only need fresh fruit and pie dough to re-create this classic and easy-to-make American treat filled with warm homemade jam. I've mixed in a bit of lime to create a light flavor note reminiscent of strawberry limeade.

Prepare the Homemade Pie Crust dough, wrap it in plastic wrap, and chill it for about 1 hour. You can also refrigerate the dough and filling overnight, then assemble the hand pies the next day.

The filling can be made the day before or while the dough is resting in the fridge. Prepare the filling by combining the strawberries, sugar, and lime zest in a large saucepan over medium heat. Bring the mixture to a simmer and cook it for 3 to 4 minutes.

Meanwhile, use a fork to stir together the lime juice, vanilla, cornstarch, and flour in a small bowl. Pour the lime juice mixture into the saucepan and cook the filling for 2 to 3 minutes, stirring it constantly, until the mixture resembles strawberry jam. Transfer the filling to a medium bowl and chill it in the fridge for 2 hours to allow the filling to cool and thicken.

Make the ginger sugar by whisking together the sugar and ginger in a shallow medium bowl. Set the topping aside.

After the dough and filling have chilled, it's time to assemble and fry your hand pies. Lightly dust a work surface with flour. Remove the dough from the fridge and place it on the prepared work surface. Weigh and cut the dough in half. Take one half and roll it out until it is ⅛ inch (3 mm) thick. Using a 5-inch (13-cm)-diameter cup, biscuit cutter, or mini tart pan, cut out six dough circles. Any scrap dough can be rolled out again and cut into more circles.

(CONTINUED)

MINI STRAWBERRY-LIME PIES (CONTINUED)

Wet your fingertip with cold water and gently run it along the outer edges of each circle. The cold water is used as the sealant that helps the dough close around the filling. Place 2 heaping tablespoons (23 g) of the filling in the center of each dough circle. Carefully fold each dough circle to create a half circle. Make sure not to squeeze any filling toward the edges of the dough, which could cause the hand pie to burst open while frying. Use your fingertips to crimp the edges in order to seal the filling inside the dough. Finally, take the tines of a fork and press the crimped edges for an additional seal. Repeat these steps with the remaining half of the dough.

Line a large baking sheet with parchment paper. Place the filled hand pies on the prepared baking sheet. Refrigerate the hand pies for 10 to 15 minutes. Cold pie dough will prevent the pies from bursting and help them hold their shape while they are frying.

To fry your hand pies, fill a medium cast-iron skillet or Dutch oven with 3 inches (8 cm) of the oil. Heat the oil to 350°F (180°C). Exact temperature is important here, so place a candy thermometer in the oil to help you keep an eye on the temperature. The cold hand pies may cause the oil temperature to drop, while oil that is too hot will burn them. Line a rimmed large baking sheet with paper towels and place it near the stove. Set a wire rack on the prepared baking sheet.

Remove the chilled hand pies from the fridge and place the baking sheet next to the frying station. Using a flat rubber spatula, carefully slide two to three hand pies into the hot oil. Cook the hand pies for 1 minute, flip them, and cook them for 1 minute on the other side. The dough should become light and golden in color. Transfer the fried hand pies to the wire rack and let any excess oil drain onto the paper towels.

Allow the hot hand pies to cool for about 1 minute. Then carefully take one pie at a time and place it in the bowl of ginger sugar. Softly flip the hand pie to coat it in the ginger sugar. Alternatively, you can sprinkle the hand pies generously with the ginger sugar. Transfer the coated pies to a serving dish and serve them warm.

PUCKER UP KEY LIME PIE

YIELDS
8 to 10 servings

CRUST

1 cup (120 g) graham cracker crumbs, packed

1 cup (120 g) gingersnap cookie crumbs, packed

⅓ cup (73 g) light brown sugar

1 tsp fresh Key lime zest

5 tbsp (70 g) unsalted butter, melted and slightly cooled

FILLING

2 (14-oz [420-ml]) cans sweetened condensed milk

½ cup (120 ml) plain or vanilla yogurt

1 cup (240 ml) fresh Key lime juice

1½ tbsp (9 g) fresh Key lime zest

1 tbsp (8 g) all-purpose flour

¼ tsp ground ginger

The citrusy, aromatic burst of Key limes pairs perfectly with a buttery, ginger cookie crust in this recipe. The beginning of June is when these green beauties come into season, and summer afternoons are made so much sweeter with a slice of this creamy tart. My mom always served her lime pies with whipped cream or toasted meringue, but I like them plain and super limey. I've become quite partial to this eggless version, which is served very cold. This is a simple recipe that will have you dreaming of the Florida Keys.

Let's start this Key lime pie by making and partially baking the crust. Preheat the oven to 350°F (180°C). Set out a 9-inch (23-cm) pie pan.

Place the graham cracker crumbs and gingersnap cookie crumbs in a medium bowl. Stir in the brown sugar and lime zest. Next, pour the melted butter over the crumbs and mix the ingredients with a fork to combine them.

Transfer the crust mixture to the pie pan and gently press it into the bottom and sides of the pan using the bottom of a measuring cup or the back of a spoon. Neatly pack the crumbs into a border at the top of the pie pan. They may be a bit crumbly, but that's okay. Place the pan on the oven's middle rack and bake it for 9 minutes, until it is set, fragrant, and a rich golden color. Place the pie pan on a wire rack to cool while you prepare the filling.

Make the filling while the crust cools. Using a hand mixer, whisk together the condensed milk, yogurt, lime juice, lime zest, flour, and ginger in a large bowl. Pour the filling into the cookie crust. Place the filled pie in the oven and bake it for 15 to 18 minutes, until the filling has just set and is no longer jiggly in the center.

Remove the pie from the oven and place it on a wire rack to completely cool. Then transfer it to the fridge and chill it for 4 hours, or up to overnight. Traditional Key lime pies are served frozen, so I like to freeze my pie for about 15 minutes before slicing and serving it.

NOTE

Use fresh Key limes for the best flavor; don't skimp and use standard limes or bottled juice.

SALTED HONEY BUTTERMILK PIE

YIELDS

8 to 10 servings

CRUST

1 (9" [23-cm]) Homemade Pie Crust (page 10)

All-purpose flour, as needed

EGG WASH

1 large egg

1 tsp water

FILLING

1¼ cups (284 g) unsalted butter, melted and cooled

¾ cup (180 ml) wildflower honey

¾ cup (150 g) sugar

¼ cup (38 g) yellow cornmeal

1 tbsp (6 g) fresh lemon zest

¼ tsp sea salt

3 large eggs, at room temperature

1 large egg yolk, at room temperature

¾ cup (180 ml) full-fat buttermilk, at room temperature

1 tsp pure vanilla extract

½ tsp pure lemon extract

GARNISHES

Flaky sea salt

Bee pollen

Fresh honeycomb

If you're not using honey and buttermilk in your pies, it's time to start. Buttermilk tends to replace whole milk in most southern recipes, and there's a good reason. The tanginess and texture it offers to a custard pie is truly unforgettable. Add some local fresh honey for that true southern pie flavor. This pie reminds me of walking through the edges of fields barefoot, sucking on honeysuckle in the summer and spreading chunks of honeycomb on warm buttered bread. So many of my fondest memories involve honey, I'm surprised I never became a beekeeper.

Since this honey buttermilk pie has a custard filling, I like to partially bake the pie crust first. Make sure your Homemade Pie Crust dough has chilled and is ready to go.

Position the oven's rack in the lower third of the oven. Preheat the oven to 425°F (220°C).

Lightly dust a work surface with flour. Set a 9-inch (23-cm) nonstick metal pie pan within arm's reach of the prepared work surface. Roll out the dough until it is ⅛ inch (3 mm) thick and about 13 inches (33 cm) in diameter. Lift the pie dough and lower it into the pie pan. Gently press the dough into the pie pan with the pads of your fingertips. Gently tuck any overhanging dough under itself and crimp the edges. Prick the bottom and sides of the pie crust that touch the pan several times with a fork.

Make the egg wash. Use a fork to beat together the egg and water in a small bowl. Lightly brush the egg wash onto the crust's crimped edges with a pastry brush. Place the pie crust in the freezer for 30 minutes to allow the dough to chill and become firm. Remember, we like super cold pie crust to go into the oven.

Remove the frozen pie crust and line the bottom of the crust with overhanging aluminum foil or parchment paper. Fill the pie crust with pie weights, dried rice, or uncooked beans. Make sure to distribute the pie weights all the way to the crimped edges to help weigh down the crust.

(CONTINUED)

Salted Honey Buttermilk Pie (Continued)

Bake the pie crust for 15 to 17 minutes, until the edges are light golden brown. Remove the pie crust from the oven and, wearing oven mitts, carefully lift the parchment paper filled with pie weights from the pie pan. Place the unfilled pie crust back in the oven and bake it for 4 minutes. Remove the pie crust from the oven and transfer it to a wire rack.

While the partially baked crust is cooling, reduce the oven's temperature to 325°F (165°C) and prepare the filling. In a large bowl, whisk together the butter and honey until they are smooth. Add the sugar, cornmeal, lemon zest, and salt. Whisk the mixture again until the ingredients are smooth.

In a small bowl, whisk together the eggs, egg yolk, buttermilk, vanilla, and lemon extract until the ingredients are smooth. Pour the egg-buttermilk mixture into the honey-sugar mixture and whisk again until the two are just combined.

Pour the filling into the partially baked crust. Tap the pie pan on the counter a few times to release any air bubbles in the filling. Place the pie on a baking sheet. Bake the pie on the oven's middle rack for 60 to 65 minutes, until the edges of the pie are set and only the center of the filling is slightly jiggly. Remove the pie from the oven and place it on a wire rack. Allow the buttermilk pie to cool for about 2 hours, until it has cooled completely to room temperature. Lightly cover the pie with aluminum foil, and then refrigerate it for 1 to 2 hours. Once the pie has completely chilled and set, top it with a sprinkling of flaky sea salt and a few pieces of bee pollen. Serve the pie chilled with fresh honeycomb.

CAROLINA MUSCADINE APPLE PIE

YIELDS

8 to 10 servings

CRUST

2 (9" [23-cm]) Homemade Pie Crusts (page 10)

All-purpose flour, as needed

Sparkling sugar, as needed

FILLING

3 cups (453 g) muscadine grapes

6 tbsp (78 g) granulated sugar, divided

3 tbsp (45 ml) fresh lemon juice

¾ cup (165 g) light brown sugar

2 tbsp (16 g) all-purpose flour

¼ cup (32 g) cornstarch

½ tsp kosher salt

¾ tsp ground cinnamon

¼ tsp ground allspice

¼ tsp ground cardamom

2 tbsp (28 g) unsalted butter

5 Granny Smith apples, peeled, cored, and thickly sliced

1 tsp pure vanilla extract

EGG WASH

1 large egg

1 tsp water

This pie represents the transition from summer to fall, when apples are plentiful and muscadine grapes are heavy on the vine. These two fruits ripen between September and October, and remind me of sitting barefoot on the kitchen floor with a big bowl of juicy muscadines, eagerly popping the pulps into my mouth, or walking into my childhood kitchen to smell a hot apple pie cooling on the counter. The tartness of Granny Smith apples marries so nicely with the sweet grapes and spices. Every bite tastes like an eastern Carolina memory.

Carolina Muscadine Apple Pie requires a top and bottom crust. You will first need to prepare the Homemade Pie Crust, divide the dough into two disks, wrap each disk in plastic wrap, and refrigerate each disk for 1 hour. Remove one of the disks from the fridge and lightly dust a work surface with flour. Roll out the dough until it is ⅛ to ¼ inch (3 to 6 mm) thick. Transfer the dough to a 9-inch (23-cm) nonstick metal pie pan, and fit the dough into the pan with your fingers. Fold the overhanging dough underneath itself and gently press the dough into the pie pan with the pads of your fingertips. Refrigerate the dough-lined pan while you prepare the filling.

Preparing the muscadine grapes for the filling takes a little time, but it's worth it. First, you need to separate the pulp from the skins. Gently squeeze each grape until the skin slides off. Set the skins in a bowl for later. Place the grape pulp, 2 tablespoons (26 g) of the granulated sugar, and lemon juice in a large saucepan over medium heat. Bring the mixture to a simmer and cook it for 8 to 10 minutes, until it has softened and the grapes have begun to release their juices. Turn off the heat and allow the mixture to cool completely.

Next, strain the seeds from the muscadine pulp mixture using a fine-mesh sieve. Discard the seeds and transfer the pulp and the reserved skins to a blender or food processor. Pulse the pulp and skins until they are the consistency of applesauce. Set this grape mixture aside while you prepare the apples.

In a medium bowl, whisk together the remaining 4 tablespoons (52 g) of granulated sugar, brown sugar, flour, cornstarch, salt, cinnamon, allspice, and cardamom.

(CONTINUED)

Carolina Muscadine Apple Pie (Continued)

Next, melt the butter in a medium saucepan over medium heat. Add the sliced apples to the butter and cook them for 2 to 3 minutes, until they have softened.

Sprinkle the sugar mixture over the apple slices, then gently fold the apples with a rubber spatula to coat them evenly in the sugar and spices. Add the grape puree and vanilla to the apples. Cook the filling for 2 to 3 minutes. Remove the filling from the heat and let it cool completely.

To make the egg wash, use a fork to beat together the egg and water in a small bowl. Set it aside.

Grab the chilled bottom pie crust from the refrigerator. Transfer the cooled filling to the crust. Brush egg wash on the outer rim of the bottom crust to help seal the top crust.

Roll out the second disk of dough until it is ⅛ to ¼ inch (3 to 6 mm) thick. Lay the top crust over the filling and cut a few small slits in the center of the dough. Press the top crust into the lower crust. Tuck any excess dough under itself and crimp the edges. Brush the top crust and the edges of the pie with egg wash, and then sprinkle the pie with the sparkling sugar. Or if you prefer to make a lattice topping, cut your top crust dough into strips of your desired width and place them across the topping.

Place the assembled pie in the freezer for 30 minutes to firm up.

Preheat the oven to 425°F (220°C). Transfer the chilled pie to a rimmed medium baking sheet to catch any hot filling that may bubble over. Place the pie in the center of the oven's middle rack. Bake the pie for 20 minutes. Reduce the temperature to 350°F (180°C) and bake the pie for 35 to 40 minutes, until the filling is bubbly and the crust is golden brown.

Place the pie on a wire rack. Allow the pie to cool for at least 2 hours before serving it. Hot filling will be a little runny, but cooled filling will be nice and firm.

NOTE

If you can't find muscadine grapes, simply swap them for sweet red seedless grapes. Slice the grapes in half and proceed directly with cooking them as directed in the recipe. There is no need to separate the skins from the pulp if you are using red seedless grapes.

KENTUCKY PIE

8 to 10 servings

CRUST

1 (9" [23-cm]) Homemade Pie Crust
(page 10)

All-purpose flour, as needed

EGG WASH

1 large egg

1 tsp water

FILLING

4 tbsp (56 g) unsalted butter, melted

1 cup (170 g) semisweet chocolate
chips, roughly chopped

¾ cup (165 g) dark brown sugar,
packed

2½ tbsp (20 g) all-purpose flour

¼ tsp sea salt

3 large eggs

⅔ cup (160 ml) pure maple syrup

3 tbsp (45 ml) Kentucky bourbon

2 tsp (10 ml) pure vanilla extract

½ cup (57 g) walnuts, roughly
chopped

½ cup (57 g) hazelnuts, roughly
chopped

1 cup (113 g) pecan halves

GARNISHES

Whipped cream

Chocolate shavings

**I grew up all over North Carolina, moved to Nashville, Tennessee,
and now live in Louisville, Kentucky. I've tried all sorts of delicious
chocolate, bourbon, and nut pies throughout the years—for example, my
grandmother always made pecan pie for Thanksgiving, and I love any pie
with chocolate. This recipe could be called Chocolate Pee-cann Bourbon
Nut Pie, if you want to be exact. But I'm shortening it to Kentucky Pie
to pay homage to my new state. It boasts a rich, boozy chocolate filling
packed with nuts in a flaky all-butter pie crust.**

Make sure your Homemade Pie Crust dough has chilled and is ready to go.

Position the oven rack to the lower third of the oven. Preheat the oven to
425°F (220°C).

Lightly dust a work surface with flour. Set a 9-inch (23-cm) nonstick metal pie
pan within arm's reach of the prepared work surface. Roll out the dough on
the prepared work surface until it is ⅛ inch (3 mm) thick and about 13 inches
(33 cm) in diameter. Lift the dough and lower it into the pie pan. Gently press
the dough into the pie pan with the pads of your fingertips. Gently tuck any
overhanging dough under itself and crimp the edges. Use a fork to prick the
bottom and sides of the crust that touch the pan several times.

Make the egg wash. In a small bowl, use a fork to beat together the egg and
water. Lightly coat the egg wash onto the crimped edges of the crust with a
pastry brush. Place the pie crust in the freezer for 30 minutes to allow the
dough to chill and become firm. Remember, we like a super cold pie crust to
go into the oven.

Remove the pie crust from the freezer. Line the crust with parchment paper,
making sure the paper hangs over the sides. Fill the pie with pie weights or
uncooked beans all the way to the crimped edges. Bake the pie crust for 15 to
17 minutes, until the edges are light golden brown. Carefully remove the pie
crust from the oven and, wearing oven mitts, lift the parchment paper with
the hot pie weights from the pie crust. Return the pie crust to the oven and
bake it for 4 minutes.

Remove the pie crust from the oven and transfer it to a wire rack to cool
for about 10 minutes. Reduce the oven's temperature to 350°F (180°C).
Reposition the oven's rack to the middle third of the oven. Line a medium
baking sheet with parchment paper.

(CONTINUED)

KENTUCKY PIE (CONTINUED)

Now it's time to make the filling. In a large bowl, pour the butter over the chocolate chips. Let the mixture sit for 2 to 3 minutes to allow the hot butter to mostly melt the chocolate. Stir in the brown sugar, flour, and salt to make a thick paste. Whisk in the eggs, maple syrup, bourbon, and vanilla and whisk until the ingredients are evenly combined.

Sprinkle the walnuts, hazelnuts, and pecans evenly across the bottom of the partially baked pie crust. Carefully pour the filling over the nuts and fill up the pie crust. Transfer the pie to the prepared baking sheet. Bake the pie for 45 to 50 minutes, until the edges of the filling are set and have begun to puff up. The center of the filling should have a slight jiggle but not a wave when you gently wiggle the pan. Transfer the hot pie to a wire rack. Let the pie cool for about 2 hours, until it has cooled completely to room temperature. The filling will continue to cook slightly once the pie is removed from the oven. It will also thicken as it cools. Slice and garnish your Kentucky pie with the whipped cream and chocolate shavings.

PUMPKIN AND SWEET POTATO PIE

YIELDS

8 to 10 servings

CRUST

1 (9" [23-cm]) Homemade Pie Crust (page 10)

All-purpose flour, as needed

FILLING

1 roasting pumpkin

Olive oil, as needed

Pinch plus ½ tsp sea salt, divided

1 sweet potato

2 tbsp (28 g) unsalted butter, melted and warm

¾ cup (165 g) dark brown sugar, packed

1 cup (240 ml) heavy cream

1 large egg, lightly beaten

3 large egg yolks, lightly beaten

2 tbsp (16 g) all-purpose flour

2 tsp (4 g) ground cinnamon

½ tsp ground nutmeg

½ tsp ground cloves

¼ tsp ground cardamom

2 tbsp (30 ml) caramel sauce

1 tsp pure vanilla extract

EGG WASH

1 large egg

1 tsp water

TOPPING

1 recipe Vanilla-Bourbon Marshmallows (page 87), toasted

"Would you like a slice of pumpkin or sweet potato pie?" is a very important question after a family Thanksgiving meal. I would like some of both, please. There's always sweet potato casserole topped with marshmallows and pumpkin pie topped with whipped cream, but for my combo pie there are toasted homemade Vanilla-Bourbon Marshmallows (page 87). This recipe is a flavor culmination of southern pie filling and topping, and it really is the best of both worlds. Roasting fresh seasonal sweet potato and pumpkin brings out the best flavors of these fall favorites. The smooth texture they create when blended with all those cozy spices and a little boozy sugar makes holiday dessert so much better!

There are several steps to creating this delicious pie, and each one is crucial for the full delectable experience. I suggest making the Homemade Pie Crust dough ahead of time, so that it is waiting in the fridge.

To make the filling, begin by preparing the roasted pumpkin puree and roasted sweet potato puree. Preheat the oven to 425°F (220°C). Line a rimmed large baking sheet with parchment paper. Scrape the seeds and stringy pulp from the baking pumpkin. Drizzle the flesh with the oil and season it with a pinch of the salt. Place the pumpkin, flesh side up, on the baking sheet. Next, pierce the skin of the sweet potato all over with a fork. Set the sweet potato on the baking sheet and bake both the pumpkin and sweet potato for 45 to 60 minutes, until each one is tender. Set the pumpkin and sweet potato on a wire rack to completely cool.

Once the pumpkin and sweet potato have cooled, scrape out the flesh from both. Puree each separately in a food processor. Then measure 1 cup (244 g) of puree of each. You may have some puree left over, which you can refrigerate to use in another recipe or to make another pie.

Place the pumpkin puree, sweet potato puree, butter, and brown sugar in a blender or food processor. Blend the ingredients until the mixture is smooth. Set the mixture aside while you partially bake your pie crust.

(CONTINUED)

PUMPKIN AND SWEET POTATO PIE (CONTINUED)

Keep the oven heated to 425°F (220°C). Lightly dust a work surface with flour. Set a 9-inch (23-cm) nonstick metal pie pan within arm's reach of the prepared work surface. Roll out the dough on the prepared work surface until it is ⅛ inch (3 mm) thick and about 13 inches (33 cm) in diameter. Lift the dough and lower it into the pie pan. Gently press the dough into the pie pan with the pads of your fingertips. Gently tuck any overhanging dough under itself and crimp the edges. Use a fork to prick the bottom and sides of the crust that touch the pan several times.

Make the egg wash. In a small bowl, use a fork to beat together the egg and water. Lightly coat the egg wash onto the crimped edges of the crust with a pastry brush. Place the pie crust in the freezer for 30 minutes to allow the dough to chill and become firm. Remember, we like a super cold pie crust to go into the oven.

Remove the pie crust from the freezer. Line the crust with parchment paper, making sure the paper hangs over the sides. Fill the pie with pie weights or uncooked beans all the way to the crimped edges. Bake in the lower third of the oven for 15 to 17 minutes, until the edges are light golden brown. Carefully remove the pie crust from the oven and, wearing oven mitts, lift the parchment paper with the hot pie weights from the pie crust. Return the pie crust to the oven and bake it for 4 minutes.

Remove the pie crust from the oven and place it on a wire rack to cool for about 10 minutes.

Now that the pumpkin and sweet potato purees and pie crust are ready, reduce the oven's temperature to 375°F (190°C). Reposition the oven's rack to the middle third of the oven. Line a medium baking sheet with parchment paper.

Make the filling by whisking together the heavy cream, egg, egg yolks, flour, cinnamon, nutmeg, cloves, cardamom, remaining ½ teaspoon of salt, caramel sauce, and vanilla in a medium bowl. Combine the cream mixture and pumpkin and sweet potato purees in a large blender and blend until everything is smooth. I have found this is a reliable method for creating a silky smooth texture.

Transfer the filling to the cooled partially baked pie crust and place the pie pan on the prepared baking sheet. Bake the pie for 40 to 45 minutes, until the outer edges of the pie filling are set and the very center has a slight wobble. If there is a wave or big ripple when you nudge the pie pan, bake the pie for 8 to 10 minutes more. Don't rush the cooking process.

Remove the pie from the oven and place it on a wire rack. Let this pie cool for 2 to 3 hours, until it has cooled completely to room temperature. Refrigerate the pie for 1 to 2 hours, or overnight, to allow it to firm up. Before serving the pie, top it with the toasted Vanilla-Bourbon Marshmallows.

NOTE

To prevent the crust from overbrowning, loosely cover the pie with aluminum foil at the 30-minute mark.

THANKSGIVING HAND PIES

CRANBERRY SAUCE

3 cups (339 g) fresh cranberries

1 cup (200 g) sugar

½ cup (120 ml) red wine

½ habanero pepper, seeds removed

3 tbsp (45 ml) sourwood honey

CRUST

1 Herb and Cheese Galette Crust (page 12)

All-purpose flour, as needed

FILLING

1 lb (454 g) cooked turkey breast or leftover holiday turkey, shredded or cut into 1" (3-cm) pieces

8 oz (224 g) Camembert cheese, cut into 1" (3-cm) pieces

EGG WASH

1 large egg

1 tsp water

TOPPING

Sea salt

Sesame seeds

Leftover holiday turkey usually turns into sandwiches or a casserole the next day, but I love making little hand pies instead: a flaky herb and cheese crust filled with turkey breast, spicy cranberry sauce, and Camembert cheese to be exact. After years of congealed or lumpy cranberry sauce debates at my aunt's holiday table, I finally decided to make my own. Sweet and tart with just a bit of heat at the end, my sauce blends nicely with the complex flavors of Camembert cheese. These individual pies are a great lunch option over plain sandwiches the day after your holiday celebrations.

Make the cranberry sauce first, since it needs time to cool. Begin by placing the cranberries, sugar, wine, and habanero pepper in a large saucepan over medium-high heat. Bring the mixture to a boil and cook for 2 to 3 minutes, watching it closely, until the sugar has turned to liquid. Stir the sauce gently with a wooden spoon as needed to keep the ingredients evenly distributed. Reduce the heat to medium-low, add the honey, and simmer the sauce for 15 minutes; the cranberries will burst and soften as they cook. Remove the habanero pepper from the saucepan and transfer the cranberry sauce to a medium bowl. Let the sauce cool for about 20 minutes, until it has cooled completely to room temperature. Don't worry if it seems a little thin while it's hot—the mixture will thicken as it cools. Cover the bowl with plastic wrap and refrigerate the sauce for at least 1 hour to cool and thicken. This sauce can also be made the day before and stored in the fridge until you are ready to assemble the hand pies.

While the cranberry sauce is chilling, make the Herb and Cheese Galette Crust, then cover it in plastic wrap and set it in the fridge to chill for 1 hour. This dough can also be made the day before and stored in the fridge until you are ready to make the hand pies. If it's super firm, allow the dough to sit at room temperature for 30 minutes before rolling it out.

When you're ready to make the hand pies, preheat the oven to 425°F (220°C). Line two rimmed medium baking sheets with parchment paper. Lightly dust a work surface with flour. Remove the crust from the fridge and place it on the prepared work surface. Cut the dough in half and roll out each half until it is ⅛ inch (3 mm) thick. Using a 5-inch (13-cm)-diameter cup or biscuit cutter, cut out six dough circles. Any scrap dough can be rolled out again and cut into more circles.

(CONTINUED)

THANKSGIVING HAND PIES (CONTINUED)

To assemble the hand pies, cover the center of each dough circle with two to three 1-inch (2.5-cm) strips of the turkey, one piece of the Camembert cheese, and 1 tablespoon (15 g) of the cranberry sauce. The filling should create a mound, but you should still be able to fold the dough over into a half circle.

Make the egg wash. Use a fork to beat together the egg and water in a small bowl. Using a pastry brush, lightly apply a thin coating of egg wash around the outer edges of each dough circle. Carefully fold the dough over to create a half circle. Make sure not to squeeze any of the filling out toward the edges. Use your fingertips to crimp the edges and seal the filling inside. Use the tines of a fork to press the crimping, creating an additional seal.

Lay six hand pies on each prepared baking sheet. Make two small slits in the center of each pie with a sharp knife. Using the pastry brush, apply a thin coating of egg wash to the top and sides of each hand pie. Top the hand pies by sprinkling them with the salt and sesame seeds. Place the baking sheets in the fridge for 10 minutes to allow the hand pies to chill. The hand pies will hold their shape much better if the dough is cold and firm before it goes into the oven.

Place the baking sheets on the oven's middle rack and bake the hand pies for 20 minutes, or until the pastry is golden brown. Set the baking sheets on a wire rack to allow the hand pies to cool for 8 to 10 minutes. Serve the hand pies warm with your favorite leftover holiday sides.

NOTE

I use a mini tart pan to cut out the dough circles.

SUMMER TOMATO GALETTE

YIELDS

8 to 10 servings

CRUST

1 Herb and Cheese Galette Crust
(page 12)

All-purpose flour, as needed

FILLING

2 to 3 heirloom tomatoes, cut into
⅛ to ¼" (3- to 6-mm)-thick slices

½ tsp sea salt, plus more as needed

1 tbsp (14 g) unsalted butter

1 cup (52 g) roughly chopped yellow
onion

2 cloves garlic, minced

½ tsp minced fresh thyme

½ tsp minced fresh parsley

¼ tsp freshly ground black pepper

2 large egg yolks

6 oz (168 g) creamy goat cheese

1 cup (84 g) grated hoop cheese

3 tbsp (27 g) cornmeal

EGG WASH

1 large egg

1 tsp water

SEED MIXTURE

1 tbsp (8 g) chia seeds

1 tbsp (9 g) sesame seeds

½ tsp garlic powder

1 tsp coarse sea salt

Sun-ripened, right-off-the-vine tomatoes from my father's garden line the window of my mother's kitchen all season long. Tomatoes were never in short supply and seemed to multiply overnight. Therefore, I grew up eating my weight in white-bread tomato sandwiches with mayonnaise and pepper, a simple concoction that tastes amazing with warm homegrown tomatoes. Occasionally I would add a thick slice of hoop cheese purchased from a local farmer's stand. Hoop cheese, a red-ring cheese that's made only from cow's milk, has a soft texture with a subtle nutty flavor. This galette is an ode to the flavors of my childhood summers, abundant in tomatoes and cheese from local dairies.

Start this recipe by making the Herb and Cheese Galette Crust. Cover it in plastic wrap and set it in the fridge to chill for 1 hour.

To prepare the filling, line a large tray with paper towels. Place the tomato slices on the paper towels, then sprinkle the tomatoes lightly with salt to help them release their juices. Let the tomatoes rest for at least 10 minutes—this is an important step to prevent a soggy galette.

Melt the butter in a medium skillet over medium-high heat. Add the onion, garlic, thyme, parsley, the ½ teaspoon of salt, and black pepper. Cook the mixture for 3 to 4 minutes, until the onion has just softened and become translucent. Transfer the mixture to a large bowl and let it cool completely.

In a small bowl, stir together the egg yolks and goat cheese until the mixture is smooth. Add the egg yolk–cheese mixture to the onion mixture and stir everything together. Mix in the hoop cheese and set the filling aside while you roll out the galette dough.

Lightly dust a work surface with flour. Line a large baking sheet with parchment paper. Remove the galette dough from the fridge, and place it on the prepared work surface. Roll out the dough to a ¼-inch (6-mm)-thick circle that is about 12 inches (30 cm) in diameter. Transfer the dough to the prepared baking sheet.

Make the egg wash. In a small bowl, use a fork to beat together the egg and water. Set the egg wash aside. Mix the seed mixture ingredients into a bowl and set aside.

(CONTINUED)

Summer Tomato Galette (Continued)

Lightly sprinkle the cornmeal across the center of the dough circle, leaving a 1-inch (2.5-cm) border of dough free of cornmeal. This cornmeal will help absorb liquid from the tomatoes and prevent the bottom of the galette crust from getting soggy. Spoon the filling onto the cornmeal-dusted dough and carefully spread the filling into an even layer with a small rubber spatula. Arrange your tomato slices across the filling in an overlapping, even single layer. Fold the edges of the dough inward toward the center, lightly covering the edges of the tomatoes and adding pleats with each turn. Secure the dough folds together by brushing a little cold water between them and pressing down on them with your fingers. The dough should resemble a pizza crust with pleats.

Brush the outer crust with a coating of the egg wash and generously sprinkle with the seed mixture: the chia seeds, sesame seeds, garlic powder, and salt. Refrigerate the galette for 15 minutes to chill the dough before baking it.

While the galette is chilling, preheat the oven to 400°F (200°C). Place the baking sheet on the oven's middle rack and bake the galette for 35 to 40 minutes, until the crust is golden brown and the filling is bubbling slightly where the cheese is melting. Place the baking sheet on a wire rack and let the galette cool for 10 minutes. Slice the galette and serve it warm.

BLACK AND BLUE BERRY COBBLERS

YIELDS

4 (4" [10-cm]) cobblers

FILLING

2½ cups (475 g) ripe fresh blueberries

2 cups (380 g) ripe fresh blackberries

1 cup (200 g) granulated sugar

¼ cup (31 g) all-purpose flour

3 tbsp (24 g) cornstarch

2 tbsp (30 ml) fresh lemon juice

1 tsp pure vanilla extract

1 tbsp (15 ml) pure maple syrup

STREUSEL TOPPING

1¼ cups (156 g) all-purpose flour

⅓ cup (67 g) granulated sugar

¾ tsp baking powder

¼ tsp baking soda

¼ tsp kosher salt

2 tsp (4 g) ground cinnamon

¼ cup (57 g) unsalted butter, cold and cut into small cubes

⅓ cup (80 ml) plus 1 tbsp (15 ml) full-fat buttermilk, cold

Turbinado sugar, as needed

Vanilla ice cream, to serve

Every year, I walk through rows of blackberry and blueberry vines early in the morning, grabbing handfuls of these little jewels to take back to my kitchen. When you don't have time to make pie crust and you're craving berry goodness, cobbler is always the southern way to go. Individual streusel-topped black and blue cobblers have all the essence of berry season, served hot with a big ole dollop of vanilla ice cream.

Preheat the oven to 400°F (200°C). Set out four 4-inch (10-cm) ramekins. Line a rimmed medium baking sheet with parchment paper.

Make the filling by placing the blueberries and blackberries in a large bowl. Sprinkle the granulated sugar and flour on top of the berries. In a small cup, use a fork to stir together the cornstarch, lemon juice, vanilla, and maple syrup. Pour the syrup mixture over the berries and then fold everything together with a rubber spatula to evenly coat the berries. Transfer the filling to a large skillet and cook the mixture over medium-low heat for 4 to 5 minutes. Slowly and constantly stir the mixture with a rubber spatula to keep it from sticking to the skillet. The filling should thicken as the berries start to break down. Remove the skillet from the heat and evenly divide the filling among the ramekins.

Next, make the streusel topping. In a medium bowl, whisk together the flour, granulated sugar, baking powder, baking soda, salt, and cinnamon. Add the butter and work it into the flour with your hands until it resembles cornmeal. Pour in the buttermilk and stir the ingredients until they are just mixed together and chunky.

Cover the filling in each ramekin with a generous layer of the streusel topping. Sprinkle the top of the streusel with the turbinado sugar. If you have leftover streusel, just spread it on a baking sheet lined with parchment paper and bake it separately for 15 to 18 minutes for a delicious snack that pairs well with fruit and yogurt.

Place the ramekins on the prepared baking sheet to catch any drippings. Bake the cobblers on the oven's middle rack for 16 to 18 minutes, until the filling is bubbling and the streusel is golden brown. Remove the baking sheet from the oven and place it on a wire rack for 10 minutes. Set the individual cobbler ramekins on a serving plate and top the cobblers with vanilla ice cream.

NOTE

To make this a large single cobbler, use a 9 x 13–inch (23 x 33–cm) or 9 x 9–inch (23 x 23–cm) ceramic baking dish. Bake the cobbler, lightly covered with aluminum foil, for 24 to 28 minutes. The filling should be bubbling and the streusel should be golden brown.

CHERRY-PLUM SKILLET COBBLER

YIELDS

6 to 8 servings

½ cup (114 g) unsalted butter, sliced into 1" (3-cm) squares

1 cup (125 g) plus 2 tbsp (16 g) all-purpose flour

½ cup (100 g) granulated sugar

½ packed cup (110 g) light brown sugar

2 tsp (10 g) baking powder

½ tsp kosher salt

1 tsp ground cinnamon

1 cup (240 ml) whole milk, at room temperature

1 tsp pure vanilla extract

½ tsp pure almond extract

1 tbsp (15 ml) Kentucky bourbon

2 tsp (4 g) fresh orange zest

2 cups (280 g) fresh bing cherries, stems and pits removed and cut in half

2 cups (308 g) ¼" (6-mm)-thick slices fresh red plums

Turbinado sugar, as needed

Vanilla ice cream, to serve

You're not a true southerner if you don't absolutely love hot fruit cobbler with vanilla ice cream. As I was growing up, my family always enjoyed homemade peach cobbler and fresh bing cherry pies. I wanted to make a version of these traditional desserts by using another favored stone fruit: juicy red plums. The blend of bourbon, red plums, and sweet cherries paired with a golden crust is the ideal dessert to help you transition from summer to fall. Because this cobbler is baked in a cast-iron skillet, there's a little crispiness to the edges, creating an additional layer of texture. Whether you serve your cobbler in a separate bowl or just eat it straight from the skillet, I know you will devour it before the ice cream melts.

It's cobbler baking time, baby! Preheat the oven to 350°F (180°C). Set out a 9- or 10-inch (23- or 25-cm) cast-iron skillet.

Place the butter in the skillet. Set the skillet in the oven to melt the butter and warm the skillet.

While the skillet is in the oven, whisk together the flour, granulated sugar, brown sugar, baking powder, salt, and cinnamon in a large bowl. In a medium bowl, whisk together the milk, vanilla, almond extract, bourbon, and orange zest. Pour the milk mixture into the flour mixture, stirring the two until they are combined.

Using oven mitts, remove the hot skillet from the oven. Pour the batter directly onto the melted butter. Scatter the cherries and plums evenly across the batter, then sprinkle everything generously with the turbinado sugar. Place the skillet back in the oven, centering it on the middle rack, and bake the cobbler for 45 to 50 minutes, until the crust has risen around the fruit and is golden brown.

Remove the skillet from the oven and set it on a wire rack to cool for about 10 minutes. Serve the cobbler warm with vanilla ice cream.

Anytime Cakes

A good cake is one that doesn't last long. When I was growing up, there was always a domed glass cake dish on the kitchen counter. I remember eagerly awaiting a finished cake to appear just so I could grab a slice, then laughing to myself every time I passed through and saw the cake shrinking in size as it was enjoyed by others.

Cakes are meant to be shared, which makes them one of my most gifted baked goods. My neighbors all know that a friendly "Hello" will soon render a wrapped slice on their doorstep. Long front-porch chats, accompanied by wine or coffee and mouthfuls of seasonal cake, are just simple southern hospitality.

Whether it's a birthday, holiday, or social gathering, there's always a good reason to mix a little flour with some sugar and slather it with a bit of frosting. The cakes in this chapter are approachable, flavorful, and perfect for every day.

TIPS FOR SUCCESS

- Make sure all your ingredients are at room temperature unless the recipe specifically calls for something hot or cold.
- When dividing batter for layer cakes, weigh the filled pans to make sure each layer will be even.
- I understand the anticipation of pulling a cake from the oven—trust me, I sometimes sit on the floor and stare at it through the oven window. But be patient and fight the urge to open your oven door too early, which will release all the heat and result in a collapsed cake.
- All unfrosted cakes can be stored in an airtight container at room temperature. Anything frosted should be kept in the fridge.

ROSEMARY-CORNMEAL POUND CAKE

YIELDS

10 to 12 servings

CAKE

2½ cups (313 g) cake flour

½ cup (75 g) yellow cornmeal

1 tsp baking powder

½ tsp kosher salt

1 cup (227 g) unsalted butter, softened

2 cups (400 g) sugar

½ cup (114 g) vegetable shortening

3 tbsp (45 ml) wildflower honey

5 large eggs

2 tbsp (30 ml) fresh lemon juice

1 tbsp (6 g) lemon zest

2 tsp (10 ml) pure vanilla extract

1 cup (240 ml) sour cream, at room temperature

2 tbsp (6 g) finely chopped fresh rosemary

HONEY GLAZE

¼ cup (60 ml) wildflower honey, warmed

4 tbsp (56 g) unsalted butter, melted

Pinch of sea salt

Cornmeal isn't just for cornbread—it makes a tasty cake too! I've tweaked my great-grandmother's pound cake to create a variation that's a bit lighter, honey-sweetened, and infused with fresh rosemary. Maybe you've noticed I'm a big honey fan, but I'm equally in love with rosemary. It's the first herb that I plant every year. I'm obsessed with its aroma, taste, and ability to transform a recipe. With fresh-from-the-garden rosemary, this is a great everyday and every-season cake.

Preheat the oven to 350°F (180°C). Spray a 10 x 3¼–inch (25 x 9–cm) Bundt cake pan with nonstick baking spray.

To make the cake, whisk together the flour, cornmeal, baking powder, and salt in a large bowl. Set the flour mixture aside.

Place the butter and sugar in the bowl of a stand mixer fitted with a paddle attachment. Beat them together at medium speed for 2 to 3 minutes, until they are fluffy. Beat in the shortening, then scrape the sides and bottom of the bowl. Pour in the honey, then mix in 1 egg at a time until the mixture is smooth. Next, add the lemon juice, lemon zest, and vanilla, mixing again until the ingredients are incorporated.

With the mixer at low speed, add one-third of the flour mixture, alternating with half of the sour cream. Repeat this process, finishing with the final one-third of the flour mixture. Be careful not to overmix the batter: Mix it just enough so that there are no visible flour streaks. Scrape the bottom and sides of the bowl as needed. Fold the rosemary into the batter until it is evenly distributed. Scoop the thick batter into the prepared Bundt cake pan and level it with a spatula. You can also spread the batter a little thicker around the outer edge, so the outer side is higher than the center. This will help the cake to rise more evenly and result in a more level bottom when inverted onto a serving plate.

Place the cake pan in the center of the oven's middle rack. Bake the cake for 55 to 65 minutes, until the exposed crust is golden brown and a toothpick inserted into the center comes out clean.

Transfer the baked cake to a wire rack to cool completely before inverting it onto a serving dish.

To make the honey glaze, stir together the honey, butter, and sea salt in a small bowl. Using a pastry brush, coat the cake with the honey glaze before slicing and serving the cake.

NEWFANGLED CARROT CAKE

CAKE

2½ cups (313 g) all-purpose flour

2 tsp (4 g) ground cinnamon

1 tsp ground ginger

1 tsp ground nutmeg

½ tsp ground cloves

¼ tsp ground allspice

½ tsp kosher salt

2 tsp (10 g) baking powder

1 tsp baking soda

1 cup (240 ml) sunflower seed oil

1½ packed cups (330 g) dark brown sugar

4 large eggs

1 large egg yolk

¾ cup (170 g) mashed ripe banana

2 tbsp (30 ml) dark amber pure maple syrup

2 tsp (10 ml) pure vanilla extract

2 cups (200 g) freshly shredded carrots

1 cup (128 g) roughly chopped dried figs

½ cup (64 g) dried sweet cherries

HONEY-MASCARPONE FROSTING

8 oz (224 g) cream cheese, at room temperature

½ cup (112 g) mascarpone cheese, at room temperature

2 tbsp (30 ml) sourwood honey

1 tbsp (15 ml) pure vanilla extract

4 cups (480 g) confectioners' sugar

Toasted walnut halves, as needed

Traditional southern carrot cake is filled with chunks of pineapple, raisins, pecans or walnuts, and heaps of shredded carrots, then coated in a thick cream cheese frosting. It's commonly served in the spring and the fall, but I love carrot cake anytime—don't you? Preferring to eat raisins in cookies and nuts as a cake topper instead of a filler, I came up with a new formula. This recipe is enhanced with dried figs and cherries and a bit of banana, with a honey-mascarpone frosting that I know you'll love. Make sure to use dark brown sugar and freshly shredded carrots for the perfect moisture level. This newfangled carrot cake is moist, delicious, and a fresh take on a beloved southern dessert.

I love a layer cake, so prepare two 9 x 2–inch (23 x 5–cm) round cake pans with a thin coating of nonstick baking spray and line the bottoms with parchment paper. Preheat the oven to 350°F (180°C).

To make the cake, whisk together the flour, cinnamon, ginger, nutmeg, cloves, allspice, salt, baking powder, and baking soda in a large bowl. Set this bowl aside. In a medium bowl, whisk together the oil, brown sugar, eggs, egg yolk, banana, maple syrup, and vanilla until the mixture is smooth.

Pour the oil mixture into the flour mixture. Using a wooden spoon or a sturdy rubber spatula, stir the two together until they are just combined. Don't overwork the batter—a few small streaks of flour are just fine. Fold in the carrots. Then fold in the figs. Finally, fold in the cherries.

Place equal amounts of the thick cake batter in the two prepared cake pans. Weigh your filled pans on a kitchen scale to make sure they're even. Place the cake pans in the center of the oven's middle rack. Bake the cakes for 45 to 55 minutes, or until a toothpick inserted into the center comes out with just a few crumbs. Remove the cake pans from the oven and place them on a wire rack to completely cool.

While the cake layers are cooling, whip up the honey-mascarpone frosting. In a large bowl, use a hand mixer to beat together the cream cheese and mascarpone cheese at medium speed until the mixture is creamy. Mix in the honey, vanilla, and confectioners' sugar at low speed until the frosting begins to thicken, then increase the speed to medium and beat the frosting for 30 seconds. Scrape the sides and bottom of the bowl with a rubber spatula, then beat the frosting again at medium speed until it is smooth.

To assemble the carrot cake, carefully invert the cake layers from their pans and peel the parchment paper off the bottoms of the cakes. Place one cake layer on your serving dish and spread half of the frosting over the top of this cake. Gently set the second cake layer on top of the frosting and cover the top of the cake with the remaining frosting. Arrange the walnut halves across the top of the cake. Slice the cake and serve it with a glass of milk or a cup of coffee.

TEATIME CAKE

YIELDS
8 to 10 servings

CAKE

1¾ cups (219 g) pastry flour

1 tsp baking powder

½ tsp baking soda

¼ tsp kosher salt

¾ cup (150 g) granulated sugar

2 large eggs

2 large egg yolks

1 tbsp (15 ml) wildflower honey

1 tbsp (15 ml) pure vanilla extract

2 tbsp (12 g) finely grated fresh orange zest

1 tbsp (6 g) finely grated fresh lemon zest

½ cup (120 ml) lemon-infused olive oil (see Note)

¾ cup (180 ml) full-fat buttermilk

ORANGE-MASCARPONE CREAM

1 cup (224 g) mascarpone cheese, at room temperature

4 tbsp (32 g) confectioners' sugar

2 tbsp (30 ml) heavy cream

2 tsp (10 ml) fresh orange juice

NOTE

I love Lucini Delicate Lemon Extra Virgin Olive Oil.

Here is a simple single-layer cake made with olive oil, buttermilk, and hints of citrus to serve at brunch, at tea parties, and on slow Sunday afternoons. Whether we're enjoying hot tea, cold sweet tea, or maybe a mimosa, we ladies like to gather for chatting, sipping, and savoring sweets. A slice of cake seems a bit more fitting for teatime than a cookie, so here we are. I love how fruity olive oil brings a unique flavor to this moist, just-sweet-enough cake. If you love a light, subtly flavored dessert to enjoy with good conversation, this is the one for you!

Preheat the oven to 350°F (180°C). Prepare an 8 x 2–inch (20 x 5–cm) round cake pan with a thin coating of nonstick baking spray. Line the bottom of the pan with parchment paper.

Make the cake first. In a small bowl, whisk together the flour, baking powder, baking soda, and salt. Set the flour mixture aside.

In a large bowl, use a hand mixer to beat together the granulated sugar, eggs, egg yolks, honey, vanilla, orange zest, and lemon zest at medium speed for 2 to 3 minutes, until the mixture is fluffy and light in color. With the mixer running at medium-low speed, slowly drizzle in the oil and mix the ingredients until the mixture is smooth.

Add half of the flour mixture to the sugar-egg mixture while continuing to beat the batter at medium-low speed. Then slowly pour in half of the buttermilk. Scrape the bottom and sides of the bowl with a rubber spatula to incorporate all the ingredients. Repeat this process with the remaining half of the flour mixture and buttermilk, mixing the batter until it is smooth.

Transfer the batter to the prepared cake pan. Lift the cake pan about 1 inch (2.5 cm) above the counter and bang it on the counter a couple of times to release any excess air bubbles.

Place the cake pan in the center of the oven's middle rack. Bake the cake for 38 to 40 minutes, or until a toothpick inserted into the center comes out with just a few crumbs. Remove the pan from the oven and place it on a wire rack to completely cool.

While the cake is cooling, make the orange-mascarpone cream. In a large bowl, use a hand mixer to beat together the mascarpone cheese, confectioners' sugar, heavy cream, and orange juice at medium speed for 1 to 2 minutes, until the cream is silky smooth.

Invert the cake pan and remove the cake, peeling away the parchment paper. Place the cake on a serving dish and spread the orange-mascarpone cream over the top. Serve slices of the cake with your favorite spirit or tea.

FRESH CHUNKY FRUIT CAKE

CAKE

1½ cups (360 ml) vegetable oil

3 large eggs

2 tsp (10 ml) pure vanilla extract

3 cups (375 g) cake flour

2 cups (400 g) granulated sugar

1 tsp baking soda

1 tsp kosher salt

1 tsp ground cinnamon

½ tsp ground ginger

2 cups (350 g) peeled, cored, and roughly chopped fresh Bosc pears

2 cups (350 g) peeled and roughly chopped Braeburn or Honeycrisp apples

1 cup (128 g) roughly chopped pitted Medjool or Deglet Noor dates

Confectioners' sugar, as needed

MAPLE CREAM FROSTING

8 oz (224 g) cream cheese, at room temperature

3 tbsp (45 ml) pure maple syrup

1 tbsp (15 ml) pure vanilla extract

1 cup (120 g) confectioners' sugar

¼ cup (60 ml) heavy cream

Right before the leaves start to fall, a quick trip to the mountains produces an abundance of fresh apples in the kitchen. Local orchards offer a wide array of apple varieties for cakes and ciders. My mother always makes an autumn bundt cake heavy with chunks of crispy, tart Braeburn apples wrapped in cozy spices. This layer-cake adaptation includes Bosc pears and dates, which are complemented by a maple cream frosting that would bring a smile to my mom's face. This is a moist, tender cake packed with fruit, and it should be enjoyed within a few days.

Preheat the oven to 350°F (180°C). Prepare two 9 x 2–inch (23 x 5–cm) round cake pans with a thin coating of nonstick baking spray. Line the bottoms of the cake pans with parchment paper.

To make the cake, combine the oil, eggs, and vanilla in a large bowl. Use a hand mixer to beat the ingredients together at medium speed for 1 to 2 minutes, until the mixture is smooth and slightly fluffy.

In a medium bowl, whisk together the flour, granulated sugar, baking soda, salt, cinnamon, and ginger. Add one-third of the flour mixture at a time to the oil mixture, combining the two with the hand mixer at medium speed. The batter will be dark golden brown and have a thick consistency resembling cookie dough. Scrape the excess batter off the hand mixer's beaters into the bowl and switch to a wooden spoon.

Using a little elbow grease, fold in the pears until they are evenly distributed. Then fold in the apples until they are evenly distributed. Finally, fold in the dates until they are evenly distributed. The moisture from the raw fruit will loosen the cake batter as you stir. Place equal amounts of the batter into the prepared cake pans and level the batter with an offset spatula. Place the cake pans in the center of the oven's middle rack. Bake the cakes for 55 to 60 minutes, or until a toothpick inserted into the center comes out with just a few crumbs. Remove the cake pans from the oven and place them on a wire rack to completely cool.

Meanwhile, make the maple cream frosting. In a large bowl, use a hand mixer to beat the cream cheese at medium speed for 2 to 3 minutes, until it is silky smooth. Mix in the maple syrup, vanilla, and confectioners' sugar at low speed for 2 to 3 minutes, until the frosting begins to thicken. Increase the speed to medium and beat the frosting for 30 seconds. Scrape the sides and bottom of the bowl with a rubber spatula. Slowly drizzle the heavy cream into the frosting while beating it at medium speed to create a spreadable consistency.

To assemble the fruit cake, carefully invert the cake layers from their pans and peel the parchment paper off the bottoms of the cakes. Place one cake layer on your serving dish and spread the maple cream frosting over the top as thickly or as thinly as you like. Gently set the second cake layer on top of the frosting and add a light dusting of confectioners' sugar before serving.

APPLE BUTTER COFFEE CAKE

CAKE

2 cups (250 g) pastry flour

1½ tsp (8 g) baking powder

½ tsp baking soda

½ tsp kosher salt

¾ cup (170 g) unsalted butter, softened

⅔ cup (133 g) granulated sugar

½ packed cup (110 g) light brown sugar

2 large eggs

1 large egg yolk

½ cup (120 ml) sour cream, at room temperature

2 tsp (10 ml) pure vanilla extract

1 cup (240 ml) full-fat buttermilk, well shaken

¾ cup (180 ml) apple butter

1 Fuji apple, peeled, cored, and thinly sliced

STREUSEL TOPPING

1¼ cups (156 g) all-purpose flour

¾ packed cup (165 g) light brown sugar

2 tsp (4 g) ground cinnamon

½ tsp kosher salt

5 tbsp (70 g) unsalted butter, melted and slightly cooled

1 tsp pure vanilla extract

Coffee cake is a delightful fall cake, and it's best enjoyed on crisp mornings while you're sipping coffee on the front porch. I also love a slice late in the evening when I'm snuggled under a blanket. Without a hint of coffee in the recipe, it gets its name from the fact that it's a great accompaniment to your cup of joe. I've added homemade apple butter and locally grown apples to this recipe for extra fall flavor. This cake tastes just like a warm hug and leaves your kitchen with the lingering scent of cinnamon apples.

Preheat the oven to 350°F (180°C). Lightly spray a 9-inch (27-cm) springform pan with nonstick baking spray.

To make the cake, whisk together the flour, baking powder, baking soda, and salt in a medium bowl. Set the flour mixture aside.

In the bowl of a stand mixer fitted with a paddle attachment, beat together the butter, granulated sugar, and brown sugar at medium-high speed for 3 to 4 minutes, until the mixture is light and fluffy. Add the eggs and egg yolk, one at a time, scraping the sides and bottom of the bowl with a rubber spatula as needed. Mix in the sour cream and vanilla until everything is combined.

Add the flour mixture and buttermilk to the butter-sugar mixture in three additions, alternating between the two and scraping the bottom and sides of the bowl between each addition. Ensure that you end this process by adding the final portion of the flour mixture. Mix the batter at low speed just until the ingredients are combined.

Transfer two-thirds of the batter to the prepared springform pan. Distribute the apple butter across the batter in small dollops. Cover the apple butter with the remaining one-third of the batter. Working in a circular clockwise pattern, place the apple slices on top of the batter to cover it with an even layer of fruit.

To make the streusel topping, whisk together the flour, brown sugar, cinnamon, and salt in a medium bowl. Pour in the butter and vanilla, then stir the ingredients with a fork to create a crumbly texture. Cover the apple slices generously with the streusel.

Place the pan on the oven's middle rack. Bake the cake for 35 to 40 minutes. Loosely cover the cake with tented aluminum foil and bake it for 20 to 25 minutes, until a toothpick inserted into the center comes out with just a few crumbs. Place the pan on a wire rack to completely cool. Remove the ring from the springform pan. Slice the cake and serve it with your favorite hot coffee.

DAD'S CHOCOLATE CAKE

CHOCOLATE GANACHE FROSTING

4 oz (112 g) dark chocolate, finely chopped

4 oz (112 g) semisweet chocolate, finely chopped

½ tsp espresso powder

¼ tsp sea salt

¼ cup (50 g) granulated sugar

½ cup (120 ml) heavy cream

½ cup (120 ml) whole milk

1 tbsp (14 g) unsalted butter

CAKE

2 cups (250 g) all-purpose flour

2 tsp (10 g) baking powder

1½ tsp (8 g) baking soda

¾ tsp sea salt

1½ cups (300 g) granulated sugar

½ cup (110 g) light brown sugar

¾ cup (64 g) Dutch-process cocoa powder

1 tsp espresso powder

2 oz (56 g) dark chocolate, roughly chopped

1 cup (240 ml) hot brewed coffee

1 tbsp (15 ml) pure vanilla extract

½ cup (114 g) unsalted butter, melted and cooled

2 large eggs

2 large egg yolks

¾ cup (180 ml) sour cream

Chocolate, chocolate, and more chocolate is what a chocolate lover's cake should be. No truer words have ever been spoken around my dad. He always requests chocolate cake each year for his birthday. This recipe is a true indulgence, made with dark chocolate, the soft tanginess of sour cream, and a rich chocolate ganache frosting. You will need a sweet tooth, a glass of milk, and an empty belly to truly enjoy this chocolate-filled experience.

Prepare the chocolate ganache first, so you can store it in the fridge while you make the cake. Place the dark chocolate, semisweet chocolate, espresso powder, salt, and granulated sugar in a medium bowl. In a small saucepan over medium heat, warm the heavy cream, milk, and butter just until the mixture is starting to bubble. Pour the hot cream mixture over the chocolate and let it rest for about 5 minutes. Whisk the mixture until it is smooth, then cover the bowl with plastic wrap and refrigerate for about 1 hour to cool and firm up slightly.

To make the cake, preheat the oven to 350°F (180°C). Prepare two 9 x 2–inch (23 x 5–cm) round cake pans with a thin coating of nonstick baking spray. Line the bottoms of the pans with parchment paper.

In a medium bowl, whisk together the flour, baking powder, baking soda, and salt. Set the flour mixture aside. In a large bowl, stir together the granulated sugar, brown sugar, cocoa powder, espresso powder, and chocolate. Pour the hot coffee into the bowl and whisk until the mixture is smooth. Pour in the vanilla and butter, and mix the ingredients with an electric hand mixer to incorporate them. Next, add the eggs and egg yolks, one at a time, mixing between each addition. Add one-third of the flour mixture while beating the batter at medium speed, and alternate the flour with ¼ cup (60 ml) of the sour cream. Scrape the bottom and sides of the bowl with a rubber spatula to incorporate all the ingredients. Repeat this process with the remaining two-thirds of the flour mixture and ½ cup (120 ml) of the sour cream until the cake batter is smooth.

Divide the batter evenly between the prepared cake pans. Place the cake pans in the center of the oven's middle rack. Bake the cakes for 38 to 40 minutes, or until a toothpick inserted into the center comes out with just a few crumbs. Remove the pans from the oven and place them on a wire rack to completely cool.

Remove the bowl of chocolate ganache frosting from the fridge. Using a hand mixer, whip the frosting at medium speed for about 2 minutes, until it is fluffy with stiff peaks.

To assemble the cake, remove the cooled cake layers from their pans by inverting them onto a flat plate. Peel away the parchment paper from the bottom of each cake layer. Place a single cake layer right side up on a serving dish. Cover the top with a layer of the chocolate ganache frosting and smooth it with an offset spatula. Repeat this process with the second layer of cake and the remaining frosting. Slice the cake and serve.

SCHMANCY 1-2-3-4 CAKE

YIELDS

10 to 12 servings

LEMON CURD

2 tbsp (12 g) fresh lemon zest

1 cup (200 g) sugar

4 large eggs, lightly beaten

½ cup (120 ml) fresh lemon juice

10 tbsp (140 g) unsalted butter, cut into ½" (1.3-cm) cubes

CAKE

2 cups (400 g) sugar

1 tbsp (6 g) fresh lemon zest

1 tbsp (6 g) fresh clementine orange zest

1 cup (227 g) unsalted butter, softened

1 tbsp (13 g) vanilla bean paste

4 large eggs

3 cups (375 g) cake flour

1 tbsp (15 g) baking powder

½ tsp kosher salt

1 cup (240 ml) whole milk

1 cup (123 g) unsalted pistachios, shells removed and roughly chopped

MERINGUE

4 large egg whites

½ tsp cream of tartar

1 cup (200 g) sugar

1 cup (240 ml) water

1 tsp pure vanilla extract

There's an old, somewhat faded cookbook in my mom's kitchen cabinet that is filled with baking recipes submitted by local women. While flipping through the pages one day, I came across a recipe for a cake with 1 cup (227 g) of butter, 2 cups (400 g) of sugar, 3 cups (375 g) of flour, and 4 eggs: The easy-to-remember 1-2-3-4 method is invaluable if you're in a jam and need to bake a cake on the fly. I wanted to give this oldie some retro flare, since it was a little lackluster in appearance. I added splashes of yellow and green with layers of homemade lemon curd and chopped pistachios, and I crowned the cake with a topping of toasted meringue. Now she's a true Dixie dessert centerpiece.

What makes this cake so special is the layers of fresh lemon curd, which needs time to chill—so it's best to make it first. Place the lemon zest and sugar in a food processor or blender and pulse until the mixture has a fine consistency. Transfer the mixture to a medium bowl and whisk in the eggs and lemon juice. Set this bowl next to the stove.

In a medium saucepan over medium-low heat, melt the butter. Slowly pour in the lemon-egg mixture, whisking to combine and continuing to whisk until the curd just starts to bubble and thicken.

Cook the lemon curd for about 10 minutes, until it starts to resemble hollandaise sauce. If it's not thickening, increase the heat to medium, but don't overcook the curd, or it will resemble scrambled eggs. Immediately remove the saucepan from the heat and strain the curd mixture through a metal sieve into a medium bowl.

Cover the bowl with plastic wrap, pressing it directly onto the curd to prevent a thick skin from forming while the curd is chilling. Refrigerate the lemon curd for 1 to 2 hours to allow it to thicken. Transfer the thickened curd to a medium glass jar with a lid to store in the fridge. Lemon curd can be made the day before you make the cake.

Now it's time to make the cake. Preheat the oven to 350°F (180°C). Prepare three 6-inch (15-cm) round cake pans with a thin coating of nonstick baking spray. Line the bottoms of the pans with parchment paper.

In the bowl of a stand mixer fitted with a paddle attachment, whisk together the sugar, lemon zest, and orange zest. Let this mixture sit for 5 minutes. Add the butter and beat the mixture at medium-high speed for 2 to 3 minutes, until it is light and fluffy. Add the vanilla bean paste and mix the ingredients again to incorporate them. Add the eggs, one at a time, scraping the bottom and sides of the bowl with a spatula as needed.

(CONTINUED)

In a medium bowl, whisk together the flour, baking powder, and salt. Mix the batter at medium-low speed while spooning in one-third of the flour mixture, alternating each flour addition with one-third of the milk until all the ingredients are combined. Scrape the bottom and sides of the bowl, then mix the batter at low speed for a few revolutions to ensure that the ingredients are thoroughly combined.

Divide the batter evenly among the prepared cake pans. Place the pans on the oven's middle rack and bake the cakes for 35 to 38 minutes, until a toothpick inserted into the center comes out with just a few crumbs. Transfer the cake pans to a wire rack to cool completely.

While the cake layers are cooling, make the meringue. Place the egg whites and cream of tartar in the bowl of a stand mixer fitted with the whisk attachment.

In a medium saucepan, combine the sugar and water, stirring them only once. Cook the sugar-water mixture over medium-low heat until the sugar has dissolved. Increase the heat to high and cook the mixture until the sugar syrup reads 240°F (116°C) on an instant-read or candy thermometer, which is between the soft-ball and firm-ball stages.

While the sugar syrup is cooking, turn on the mixer to medium speed. Whip the egg whites and cream of tartar for 1 to 2 minutes, until soft peaks form. When you lift the head of the mixer, the fluffy egg whites should form gentle peaks that slowly collapse back into the mixture.

Once the egg whites have formed soft peaks and the sugar syrup is ready, keep the mixer running at medium speed and carefully pour a slow drizzle of the hot sugar syrup into the egg whites. Aim for the space between the rotating whisk and the side of the bowl to prevent the sugar from sticking to the sides of the bowl. Add the vanilla extract and mix to incorporate.

Once the sugar syrup and vanilla have been added, increase the mixer's speed to high and whip the meringue for 5 to 6 minutes, until the desired stiff peaks have formed. The mixing bowl will be hot, so I tend to whisk until the bowl cools. Stiff peaks will hold their shape and, if you invert the bowl, they should not move. Transfer the meringue to a large piping bag with your desired piping tip, or cut a 1-inch (2.5-cm) slit at the bottom of the piping bag.

To assemble the cake, first prepare the cake layers. If the cakes' tops are not level, use a serrated knife to cut and level the tops. Place one of the cake layers on the desired serving plate or cake stand. Pipe a ring of the meringue around the edge of the cake as a border. Spoon ¼ to ⅓ cup (60 to 80 ml) of the lemon curd onto the middle of the cake layer and level the curd with an offset spatula. Sprinkle ½ cup (62 g) of the pistachios across the curd.

Place the second cake layer gently on top of the first and repeat the preceding steps with a border of meringue, a layer of lemon curd, and a layer of pistachios. Add the third layer of cake on top. Cover the top and sides of the cake with the remaining meringue. Use an offset spatula to make as many swoops and peaks in the meringue as possible.

Use a kitchen torch to toast the meringue, constantly moving across the meringue to prevent it from burning. You want to see golden-brown highlights on the tops of the peaks. Slice and serve the cake.

DOUBLE COCONUT CUPCAKES

CUPCAKES

3 cups (375 g) cake flour

1 tsp baking powder

½ tsp baking soda

½ tsp kosher salt

1 cup (227 g) unsalted butter, softened

2 cups (200 g) granulated sugar

4 large eggs

1 large egg white

2 tsp (4 g) finely grated fresh lemon zest

1 tbsp (15 ml) pure vanilla extract

¼ tsp coconut extract

1 cup (240 ml) full-fat coconut milk

2½ cups (210 g) sweetened shredded coconut, plus more as needed

COCONUT BUTTERCREAM FROSTING

1½ cups (341 g) unsalted butter, softened

6 cups (720 g) confectioners' sugar, plus more if needed

⅓ cup (80 ml) full-fat coconut milk, plus more if needed

½ tsp coconut extract

¼ tsp sea salt

Coconut cake is commonly served in the spring at egg hunts or in the winter as a snow-inspired holiday dessert. I've seen versions of coconut layer cakes, bunny-shaped coconut cakes, and coconut sheet cakes. My great-grandmother carved out fresh whole coconuts for her coconut cake masterpiece. But I'm obsessed with frosting cupcakes, so here we are. I'm a huge coconut fan, but I don't love the large, chewy shredded coconut pieces in the cake itself. I prefer to blitz the shredded coconut into a thick powder, then fold it into my batter. A soft cupcake topped with a generous swirl of coconut frosting, lightly sprinkled with shredded coconut, is just perfect to me.

It's cupcake time! Preheat the oven to 325°F (165°C). Line two 12-cavity standard muffin pans with paper liners.

To make the cupcakes, whisk together the flour, baking powder, baking soda, and salt in a medium bowl. Set the flour mixture aside.

In the bowl of a stand mixer fitted with the paddle attachment, combine the butter and granulated sugar and beat them at medium speed for 2 to 3 minutes, until they are smooth. With the mixer running, add the eggs, one at a time. Then add the egg white. Make sure to scrape the sides and bottom of the bowl with a rubber spatula as needed to make sure everything is incorporated. Add the lemon zest, vanilla, and coconut extract, then mix the batter until the ingredients are just incorporated.

With the mixer running at medium speed, spoon one-third of the flour mixture into the bowl. Next, slowly pour in ½ cup (120 ml) of the coconut milk, mixing until the batter is smooth. Stop to scrape the bottom and sides of the bowl as needed. Repeat this process, alternating one-third of the flour mixture, the remaining ½ cup (120 ml) of coconut milk, and the final one-third of the flour mixture. Increase the mixer's speed to medium-high and mix the batter for about 30 seconds to make sure everything is well combined. Remove the bowl from the stand mixer.

Place the shredded coconut in a food processor and pulse it until the coconut has a cornmeal-like consistency. Fold the coconut powder into the cupcake batter with a rubber spatula. Scoop the batter into the prepared muffin cavities, filling them three-fourths full. Bake one pan of cupcakes at a time on the oven's middle rack for 25 to 30 minutes, until the centers of the cupcakes spring back when gently poked with your finger, or until a cake tester inserted into a cupcake's center comes out clean.

(CONTINUED)

DOUBLE COCONUT CUPCAKES (CONTINUED)

Place the muffin pans on a wire rack for about 5 minutes, until you can gently lift the cupcakes out of the cavities. Set the individual cupcakes directly on the rack to cool completely.

Meanwhile, make your coconut buttercream frosting. In the bowl of a stand mixer fitted with the paddle attachment, beat the butter for about 2 minutes at medium speed, until it is smooth and creamy. Switch to the whisk attachment. With the mixer running at low speed, add 3 cups (360 g) of the confectioners' sugar, the coconut milk, coconut extract, and salt. Increase the mixer's speed to medium-high and mix the frosting for 1 minute to blend the ingredients together. Reduce the mixer's speed to low and add 1 cup (120 g) of the confectioners' sugar at a time, increasing the mixer's speed to medium after each addition to ensure that the confectioners' sugar is incorporated. Whip the frosting for 1 to 2 minutes, until it is fluffy and smooth. If you prefer a thicker frosting, mix in 1 tablespoon (8 g) of additional confectioner's sugar at a time to thicken it. Or, if you prefer a thinner frosting, add 1 teaspoon of extra coconut milk at a time to thin the buttercream. If you find American buttercream a bit too sweet for your taste, mix in ¼ teaspoon of fine sea salt at a time, adjusting to your liking.

Scoop the coconut buttercream frosting into a piping bag fitted with a large star piping tip. Twist the open end of the bag tightly closed and gently squeeze with even pressure from both hands, always from the top of the bag. Frost the cupcakes starting on the outer edge and working inward in a clockwise direction, allowing each pass to overlap the previous one. Ending in the center of the cupcake, gently press down and lift the piping tip away from the cupcake as you release the pressure from the top of the bag. Sprinkle the cupcakes with a light or heavy snowfall of additional shredded coconut to finish.

HUMMINGBIRD BUNDT CAKE

YIELDS

10 to 12 servings

CAKE

3 cups (375 g) cake flour

1 tsp ground cinnamon

½ tsp ground allspice

¼ tsp ground anise

1 tsp baking soda

1 tsp sea salt

1 cup (224 g) coconut oil, melted and cooled

1½ cups (300 g) granulated sugar

½ cup (110 g) light brown sugar

3 large eggs, lightly beaten

2 tsp (10 ml) pure vanilla extract

8 oz (224 g) crushed pineapple, with juice

2 cups (454 g) mashed overripe banana

1 cup (113 g) roughly chopped pecans

FROSTING

½ cup (116 g) cream cheese, at room temperature

¼ cup (57 g) unsalted butter, softened

2½ cups (300 g) confectioners' sugar, plus more if needed

1 tsp pure vanilla extract

1 tsp fresh lemon juice

1 tsp milk (optional)

1 cup (113 g) roughly chopped pecans, for serving

My grandmother always baked her hummingbird cake as a Bundt cake instead of a layer cake. Hummingbird cake got its name because it's said that the dessert is sweet enough to attract hummingbirds. I love the soft notes of pineapple and banana in this recipe, with just enough frosting to sweeten the whole cake. Maybe I won't have to fight off the nectar-loving seasonal hummingbirds when I'm enjoying a slice outside!

Preheat the oven to 350°F (180°C). Choose your favorite 10- to 12-cup (2.4- to 2.9-L) Bundt pan, and spray it with a light coating of nonstick baking spray.

Next, make the cake. In a medium bowl, whisk together the flour, cinnamon, allspice, anise, baking soda, and salt. Set the flour mixture aside.

In the bowl of a stand mixer fitted with a paddle attachment, beat together the oil, granulated sugar, and brown sugar at medium speed for 1 to 2 minutes, until the mixture is smooth. Add the eggs and vanilla, scraping the sides and bottom of the bowl with a rubber spatula as needed. Add the pineapple and its juice and the banana and mix to combine the ingredients. Then, with the mixer running at medium speed, spoon in the flour mixture and beat the ingredients for 1 to 2 minutes, until a cake batter forms. Fold in the pecans with a rubber spatula to disperse them throughout the batter.

Spoon the batter into the prepared Bundt pan and place it in the center of the oven's middle rack. Bake the cake for 40 to 50 minutes, or until a toothpick inserted into the center comes out with just a few crumbs. Remove the Bundt pan from the oven and place it directly on a wire rack to completely cool.

To prepare the frosting, combine the cream cheese and butter in a large bowl. Beat them with a hand mixer for 2 to 3 minutes, until they are fluffy. Add the confectioners' sugar, vanilla, and lemon juice. Mix again for 2 to 3 minutes, until a frosting forms. For a thinner frosting, mix in the milk (if using). To thicken the frosting, add an additional ¼ cup (30 g) of confectioners' sugar, then beat the frosting again.

Place the cooled cake on a serving dish. Cover it with the frosting, then sprinkle the top with the pecans before slicing and serving it.

WHOLE LEMON CAKE

YIELDS

8 to 10 servings

CAKE

3 cups (375 g) cake flour

½ tsp baking powder

½ tsp baking soda

½ tsp kosher salt

1 cup (227 g) unsalted butter, at room temperature

2 cups (400 g) granulated sugar

¼ cup (57 g) vegetable shortening

4 large eggs

⅓ cup (80 ml) fresh lemon juice

3 packed tbsp (18 g) fresh lemon zest

1 tbsp (15 ml) pure vanilla extract

1 cup (240 ml) sour cream

LEMON GLAZE

½ cup (120 ml) fresh lemon juice

½ cup (100 g) granulated sugar

LEMON ICING

½ cup (60 g) confectioners' sugar

1 tbsp (15 ml) fresh lemon juice

EDIBLE FLOWERS

Pansies or edible flowers of choice (see Note)

NOTE

Edible flowers can be purchased online: Visit Gourmet Sweet Botanicals at gourmetsweetbotanicals.com and Marx Foods at marxfoods.com.

I've converted my great-grandmother's classic vanilla pound cake recipe into a summery lemon treat. She knew how to use shortening for that perfect pound cake texture, and now it's super zesty too. This is a decorative Bundt cake that uses fresh lemon three ways, and it's a beautiful dessert to display at all your spring and summer parties. The rich lemon cake is topped with a lemon glaze, a drizzle of lemon icing, and colorful edible flowers. If you're on Team Citrus rather than Team Chocolate, you'll be obsessed!

Preheat the oven to 325°F (165°C). Choose a decorative 10-cup (2.4-L) Bundt pan, then spray it with a thin coating of nonstick baking spray.

To make the cake, whisk together the flour, baking powder, baking soda, and salt in a medium bowl. Set the flour mixture aside.

In the bowl of a stand mixer fitted with a paddle attachment, cream together the butter and granulated sugar at medium speed for about 3 minutes, until the mixture is light and fluffy. Add the shortening and mix again. Add the eggs, one at a time, scraping the sides and bottom of the bowl with a rubber spatula as needed. Add the lemon juice, lemon zest, and vanilla, mixing again to combine the ingredients. With the mixer running at medium-low speed, spoon in one-third of the flour mixture, then add ½ cup (120 ml) of the sour cream. Scrape the bottom and sides of the bowl with a rubber spatula to incorporate all the ingredients. Repeat this process—adding one-third of the flour mixture, then the remaining ½ cup (120 ml) sour cream, then the remaining one-third of the flour mixture—being sure to scrape the bowl between each addition. Beat the batter until it is smooth.

Transfer the batter to the prepared cake pan. Place the pan in the center of the oven's middle rack. Bake the cake for 65 to 70 minutes, or until a toothpick inserted into the center comes out with just a few crumbs. Remove the cake from the oven and place the pan on a wire rack to completely cool.

To prepare the lemon glaze, combine the lemon juice and granulated sugar in a small skillet. Heat the mixture over medium heat for 2 to 3 minutes, until the sugar is dissolved. Set the lemon glaze aside.

Make the lemon icing by whisking together the confectioners' sugar and lemon juice in a small bowl until the icing is smooth. Set the lemon icing aside.

Invert the cooled cake onto a serving dish and use a toothpick to poke small holes into the grooves of the cake. Use a pastry brush to apply the glaze to the cake and over the small holes. Let the cake stand for 3 to 4 minutes to absorb the syrup, and then brush it with the glaze again. To finish, pour the lemon icing over the top and down the sides of the cake, covering any holes. Decorate the cake with the edible flowers. Slice and serve the cake with a glass of cold, fresh-squeezed lemonade if you feel like a bit more tartness.

CARAMEL SHEET CAKE

CAKE

3 cups (375 g) cake flour

1½ tsp (8 g) baking powder

½ tsp baking soda

½ tsp kosher salt

½ tsp ground cinnamon

1⅔ cups (332 g) granulated sugar

1 cup (227 g) unsalted butter, softened

2 large eggs, at room temperature

2 large egg yolks, at room temperature

¼ cup (60 g) unsweetened applesauce

2 tsp (10 ml) pure vanilla extract

1 cup (240 ml) full-fat yogurt, at room temperature

½ cup (120 ml) full-fat buttermilk, well shaken

CARAMEL FROSTING

¾ cup (170 g) unsalted butter, cut into 1" (3-cm) pieces

1½ packed cups (330 g) dark brown sugar

¾ cup (150 g) granulated sugar

⅔ cup (160 ml) heavy cream, divided

1 tsp pure vanilla extract

½ tsp fine sea salt

1 tbsp (15 ml) Kentucky bourbon

3 to 4 cups (360 to 480 g) confectioners' sugar

Flaky sea salt, as needed

Here is a twist on the classic caramel cake. Each baker's recipe differs slightly, but one thing's for sure: A vanilla cake with caramel frosting is being made somewhere in the South this very minute. Make this for a group, and be sure to have plenty of milk on hand to wash it down.

Preheat the oven to 325°F (165°C). Lightly spray a 9 x 13 x 2–inch (23 x 33 x 5–cm) sheet cake pan with nonstick baking spray. To make the cake, whisk together the flour, baking powder, baking soda, salt, and cinnamon in a medium bowl. Set the flour mixture aside.

In the bowl of a stand mixer fitted with the paddle attachment, beat together the granulated sugar and butter at medium-high speed for 2 to 3 minutes. Add the eggs, egg yolks, applesauce, and vanilla, then mix the ingredients well. Scrape down the sides and bottom of the bowl with a rubber spatula. Then beat in ½ cup (120 ml) of the yogurt. Reduce the mixer's speed to medium-low and add half of the flour mixture, then the remaining ½ cup (120 ml) of yogurt, the remaining half of the flour mixture, and finally the buttermilk. Increase the mixer's speed to medium and mix to incorporate the ingredients. Scrape the bottom and sides of the bowl with a rubber spatula, and then stir the batter once or twice with a hand whisk to make sure everything from the bottom of the bowl is mixed in. You should have a thick, velvety batter.

Pour the batter into the prepared cake pan and level the batter with an offset spatula. Place the pan on the oven's middle rack. Bake the cake for 45 to 48 minutes, rotating the pan halfway through the baking time. The cake is ready when it is light gold in color and has started to pull away from the sides of the pan. A toothpick inserted into the center should come out clean or with just a few crumbs. Transfer the cake pan to a wire rack to completely cool before frosting the cake.

To make the caramel frosting, melt the butter in a medium saucepan over medium-high heat. Add the brown sugar, granulated sugar, ⅓ cup (80 ml) of the heavy cream, the vanilla, and fine sea salt. Gently stir the mixture with a wooden spoon for 1 to 2 minutes, until the sugars have dissolved. Bring the mixture to a boil and cook it for 2 minutes. Remove the saucepan from the heat, and then carefully pour the caramel sauce into the bowl of a stand mixer fitted with the whisk attachment. Let the hot caramel sauce cool for 30 minutes. It should still be warm when you proceed to the next step. Add the remaining ⅓ cup (80 ml) of heavy cream, the bourbon, and 1 cup (120 g) of the confectioners' sugar. Mix the ingredients at medium-high speed until they are smooth. Slowly add ½ cup (60 g) of the remaining 2 to 3 cups (240 to 360 g) of confectioners' sugar at a time while continuing to mix the ingredients. The frosting will thicken as it cools, so I prefer to add just enough confectioners' sugar to make the frosting thick and spreadable but still able to drizzle when you lift the whisk from the bowl.

Spread the warm caramel frosting across the cooled cake, then sprinkle the frosting with the flaky sea salt. Slice and serve the cake.

Sweet Tooth–Satisfying Cookies and Bars

Three cookies and a glass of milk, please!

I'm pretty sure I received my raging sweet tooth and love for cookies from my father. The man can smell a warm cookie from a mile away. And I, too, have burned my mouth many times on hot cookies simply because I couldn't wait any longer for them to cool before devouring them. Maybe that's why I always have frozen cookie dough in the fridge ready for a late-night cookie craving.

Every recipe in this chapter is near and dear to my heart. The taste of freshly picked berries, the fun of evenings spent by campfires, the memories made while decorating cookies with loved ones, and the excitement of hunting ripe persimmons on the ground are all examples of why food is such an integral part of our lives. I'm sure you have a few favorite recipes that mean as much to you.

All of these cookies and bars make great gifts. They pack well in metal tins or plastic wrapping and stay fresh a bit longer than breads or pies. I suggest making a batch with a friend and then sending a few with a special note to brighten someone's day. A few homemade cookies will always bring about a smile.

TIPS FOR SUCCESS

- Make sure all your ingredients are at room temperature unless the recipe specifically calls for something hot or cold.
- Use fresh berries for jam recipes. Feel free to swap out your favorite homemade preserves if you like.
- Let your cookie dough rest and chill for the noted amount of time.
- Don't overbake your cookies and brownies; slightly underdone is best, as they will firm up as they cool.
- All baked cookies and bars can be stored in an airtight container at room temperature. Chocolate-Chai Whoopie Pies (page 98) and Mom's Persimmon Pudding Bars (page 89) should be kept in the fridge.
- Always bake with cool baking sheets. If you are using the same baking sheet for multiple batches of cookies, let it cool to room temperature between batches.

ORANGE-CHOCOLATE CHIP COOKIES

2¾ cups (344 g) all-purpose flour

1 tsp baking soda

½ tsp sea salt

1½ cups (330 g) light brown sugar

⅔ cup (133 g) granulated sugar

1 tbsp (6 g) fresh orange zest

1 cup (227 g) unsalted butter, cut into cubes

2 tsp (10 ml) pure vanilla extract

2 large eggs

1 large egg yolk

1 tbsp (15 ml) plain Greek yogurt

½ cup (85 g) roughly chopped semisweet chocolate (at least 56% cacao)

½ cup (85 g) roughly chopped German sweet chocolate (at least 48% cacao)

I'm a big fan of pairing chocolate with orange, and I'm always in the mood for a warm cookie. The combo reminds me of sharing chocolate oranges with my grandfather and finding a navel orange along with dark chocolate candies at the bottom of my Christmas stocking every year. I decided to create a cookie with a soft center, just enough sweetness, delicious chocolate flavor, and a hint of orange to reflect these citrus-cocoa childhood recollections. Using a roughly chopped baking chocolate bar instead of chips distributes little chocolate shards throughout the batter, ensuring that chocolate is in every bite!

In a medium bowl, whisk together the flour, baking soda, and salt. Set the flour mixture aside.

In a large bowl, stir together the brown sugar, granulated sugar, and orange zest.

Next, brown the butter. Place the butter in a medium, light-colored skillet over medium heat. If the skillet is dark, it will be hard to tell if the butter solids are browning. Stir the butter as it melts. It will then foam and start to sizzle. Continue to stir the butter for 5 to 7 minutes, until it starts to turn a golden-brown color. The foam will begin to dissipate and solid brown milk dots will form at the bottom of the skillet. The browned butter should have a lovely nutty aroma. Immediately transfer the browned butter to a heatproof medium bowl to prevent it from cooking any further. Let the browned butter cool.

Pour the warm browned butter into the bowl with the sugar mixture. Stir the ingredients with a rubber spatula until they are well combined and they form a paste-like consistency. Add the vanilla, eggs, egg yolk, and yogurt to the sugar paste and stir until the ingredients are combined. Switch to using a wooden spoon, since the cookie dough will start to thicken. Slowly stir half of the flour mixture into the wet sugar mixture. Once it's incorporated, add the remaining half of the flour mixture, stirring until the ingredients are incorporated. Finally, fold in the semisweet chocolate and German sweet chocolate. This is a soft cookie dough, so we will need to chill it before scooping.

Cover the bowl with plastic wrap and refrigerate the cookie dough for a minimum of 2 hours to allow it to firm up and develop its flavor.

(CONTINUED)

ORANGE–CHOCOLATE CHIP COOKIES (CONTINUED)

Preheat the oven to 350°F (180°C). Line two rimmed large baking sheets with parchment paper or silicone baking mats.

Measure out 2-tablespoon (30-g) balls of cookie dough using a cookie scoop or ice cream scoop. Roll the dough into smooth balls with your hands, and then place them 2 inches (5 cm) apart on the baking sheets. You should be able to fit about six cookies on each baking sheet. Bake the cookies on the oven's middle rack for 10 to 12 minutes, until the edges are light golden brown.

Remove the baking sheets from the oven and place them on wire racks for 5 minutes. The cookies' centers will appear underbaked—puffy and soft—but they will flatten and cook through as they cool. Don't overbake your cookies!

Gently remove each cookie from the baking sheets and place them directly on the rack to completely cool. The result should be a soft-center cookie with a slightly crispy texture on the edges.

NOTES

This cookie dough can be made a day ahead and stored in the fridge. Letting the dough sit overnight only adds more flavor.

Store the cookies at room temperature in an airtight container, or wrap them individually in plastic wrap and freeze them.

BERRY-OAT CRUMB BARS

BERRY JAM

1¼ cups (250 g) granulated sugar

1 tbsp (6 g) fresh lemon zest

½ tsp ground ginger

¼ tsp kosher salt

1 cup (190 g) fresh raspberries

2 cups (380 g) fresh blackberries

1 tsp pure vanilla extract

CRUMB BARS

1 cup (227 g) salted butter, softened

2 cups (250 g) all-purpose flour

½ cup (40 g) old-fashioned oats

1 cup (120 g) confectioners' sugar, sifted

2 tbsp (28 g) light brown sugar

½ tsp ground cinnamon

1 tsp fresh lemon zest

2 tsp (4 g) pink peppercorns, coarsely ground

1 tsp pure vanilla extract

CRUMBLE

⅓ cup (42 g) all-purpose flour

½ cup (40 g) old-fashioned oats

¼ cup (50 g) granulated sugar

2 tsp (4 g) fresh lemon zest

4 tbsp (56 g) unsalted butter, melted and cooled

Oatmeal bars are pretty much handheld cookie cobblers, don't you think? This recipe combines sweet vine-ripened raspberries and blackberries, then layers them with oatmeal shortbread and a little zing from pink peppercorns. My first dessert with pink peppercorns was a shortbread cookie, and I was immediately hooked. I wanted to re-create them with warm summer berries in a hodgepodge fruit bar. It's the best way to eat cobbler on the go. I suggest packing a few for a hike or summer picnic.

The berry jam needs time to cool, so let's make that first. In a small bowl, stir together the granulated sugar, lemon zest, ginger, and salt. Place the raspberries and blackberries in a large skillet and sprinkle the sugar mixture on top. Cook the berry mixture over medium heat for 2 to 3 minutes, stirring gently, until the sugar dissolves. Increase the heat to medium-high and bring the berry mixture to a boil. Cook it for 8 to 10 minutes, until its temperature reads 220°F (105°C) on a candy thermometer.

Remove the skillet from the heat and stir the vanilla into the berry mixture. Transfer the berry mixture to a heatproof medium bowl. Mash the berries slightly with a potato masher or a wooden spoon, making sure to leave a few chunks in the jam. Allow the jam to cool completely at room temperature, then cover the bowl with plastic wrap. Refrigerate the jam for 1 hour to allow it to thicken and chill.

To make the crumb bars, preheat the oven to 350°F (180°C). Line an 8- or 9-inch (20- or 23-cm) square baking pan with parchment paper, being sure to leave some parchment paper hanging over the sides of the pan—this will make it easier to lift the bars out of the pan after they are baked.

In the bowl of a stand mixer fitted with the paddle attachment, beat together the butter, flour, oats, confectioners' sugar, brown sugar, cinnamon, lemon zest, peppercorns, and vanilla at medium speed for 2 to 3 minutes, until a loose cookie dough forms. Reserve ¼ cup (60 g) of the mixture for the bars' topping. Transfer the remaining dough to the prepared baking pan and press it firmly into the bottom of the pan to create an even layer.

(CONTINUED)

BERRY-OAT CRUMB BARS (CONTINUED)

Place the pan on the oven's middle rack and bake the bottom crust for 13 to 15 minutes, until it is light gold. Remove the baking pan from the oven. With a fork, poke a few holes into the surface of the warm crust, then let the crust cool slightly on a wire rack. I poke a few holes to let a little bit of the jam seep into the bottom crust. This step is purely optional. Spread the berry jam on the bottom crust. Crumble the reserved oat mixture across the surface of the jam.

Make the crumble: In a small bowl, use a fork to stir together the flour, oats, granulated sugar, lemon zest, and butter. Sprinkle the crumble over the jam and oat mixture, leaving a few bare spots of jam showing through.

Return the baking pan to the oven and bake the bars for 30 to 35 minutes, until the top crumble is light golden brown. Remove the baking pan from the oven and place it on a wire rack. Allow the bars to completely cool in the pan before lifting them out by pulling up on the overhanging parchment paper. Place on a cutting board and cut it into bars. Serve the bars with extra jam or wrap each bar individually for a to-go treat.

MOLASSES OATMEAL COOKIES

YIELDS

12 large cookies

2 cups (250 g) bread flour

1 cup (80 g) old-fashioned oats

1 tsp baking powder

1 tsp baking soda

½ tsp sea salt

1 tbsp (6 g) ground ginger

2 tsp (4 g) ground cinnamon

1 tsp ground cloves

½ cup (114 g) unsalted butter, at room temperature

½ cup (110 g) dark brown sugar

⅓ cup (67 g) granulated sugar

¼ cup (85 g) unsulfured molasses

1 tsp pure vanilla extract

1 large egg

2 large egg yolks

I've burned my mouth on so many hot oatmeal cookies, you'd think I would have learned to wait until they cooled. But the few minutes of watching them through the oven window seems like forever. Chewy oatmeal cookies with fruit will always be on the top of my cookie list, but this spiced version with rich molasses is fighting for top honors. Molasses is the key ingredient for these chewy cookies, a common flavor used in everything from southern baked beans to barbecue sauce. All dishes employing molasses are pretty tasty, but my favorite way to enjoy this sugar cane product is hot out of the oven with a scoop of vanilla ice cream.

In a medium bowl, whisk together the flour, oats, baking powder, baking soda, salt, ginger, cinnamon, and cloves. Set the flour mixture aside.

In the bowl of a stand mixer fitted with the paddle attachment, beat together the butter, brown sugar, and granulated sugar at medium speed for 2 to 3 minutes, until the mixture is creamy. Scrape the sides and bottom of the bowl as needed, then pour in the molasses and vanilla. Mix the ingredients again, adding the egg and egg yolks one at a time. Spoon in the flour mixture, beating the ingredients for 1 to 2 minutes, until a cookie dough forms. Cover the bowl with plastic wrap and refrigerate the dough for 1 to 2 hours.

Preheat the oven to 350°F (180°C). Line two rimmed large baking sheets with parchment paper or silicone baking mats. Measure the cookie dough using a 2-tablespoon (30-g) scoop, then roll the dough portions into balls with the palm of your hands. Space the cookie balls 2 inches (5 cm) apart on the baking sheets, with six cookies per baking sheet.

Place one of the baking sheets on the oven's middle rack and bake the cookies for 12 to 14 minutes. The cookies will be golden brown around the edges and soft in the center. They will continue to cook as they cool, creating a chewy texture. Repeat this step with the other baking sheet of cookies.

Place the baking sheets on wire racks for 5 minutes. Then gently transfer the cookies to the racks to completely cool. Serve the cookies with vanilla ice cream.

NOTES

This cookie dough can be made a day ahead and stored in the fridge. Letting the dough sit overnight only adds more flavor.

Store the cookies at room temperature in an airtight container, or wrap them individually in plastic wrap and freeze them.

Bread flour retains liquid and has more gluten than all-purpose flour, making this cookie perfectly moist and chewy.

BLACKBERRY JAM THUMBPRINT COOKIES

YIELDS

26 cookies

BLACKBERRY JAM

1¼ cups (250 g) granulated sugar

1 tbsp (6 g) fresh orange zest

½ tsp ground cinnamon

¼ tsp kosher salt

3 cups (570 g) fresh blackberries

1 tsp pure vanilla extract

COOKIES

2¼ cups (281 g) all-purpose flour

2 tsp (6 g) cornstarch

¼ tsp kosher salt

1 cup (227 g) unsalted butter, softened

⅓ cup (67 g) granulated sugar

⅓ cup (73 g) light brown sugar

2 large egg yolks

½ tsp pure almond extract

½ tsp pure vanilla extract

CINNAMON SUGAR

¼ cup (50 g) granulated sugar

½ tsp ground cinnamon

My mom cans homemade fruit preserves every year, and I love smearing heaping spoonfuls onto cookies. Thumbprint shortbreads are the perfect vessel for these summery fruit spreads, a delightful treat where every bite has both sweet blackberries and buttery crust. Serve these at afternoon picnics, at tea parties, or for lazy-day snacks on the front porch.

First, make the blackberry jam so it has time to cool. In a small bowl, stir together the granulated sugar, orange zest, cinnamon, and salt. Place the blackberries in a large skillet and sprinkle the sugar mixture on top. Cook the berries over medium heat for 2 to 3 minutes, stirring them gently, until the sugar has dissolved. Increase the heat to medium-high and bring the berry mixture to a boil, then cook it for 8 to 10 minutes, until its temperature reads 220°F (105°C) on a candy thermometer.

Remove the skillet from the heat, stir the vanilla into the jam, and transfer the jam to a heatproof medium bowl. Mash the blackberries slightly with a potato masher or a wooden spoon; I like to leave a few chunks of berries. Let the jam cool completely at room temperature. Then cover the bowl with plastic wrap and place the jam in the fridge to thicken for 1 hour.

To make the cookies, whisk together the flour, cornstarch, and salt in a small bowl. Set the flour mixture aside. In the bowl of a stand mixer fitted with a paddle attachment, beat the butter, granulated sugar, and brown sugar together at medium speed for 2 to 3 minutes, until the mixture is creamy. Scrape the sides and bottom of the bowl as needed, then pour in the egg yolks, almond extract, and vanilla. Mix again to incorporate the ingredients. Spoon in the flour mixture, beating the ingredients on low speed for 1 to 2 minutes, until a cookie dough forms.

Preheat the oven to 350°F (180°C). Line two rimmed large baking sheets with parchment paper or silicone baking mats. While the oven preheats, make the cinnamon sugar. In a shallow bowl, stir together the granulated sugar and cinnamon. Set the cinnamon sugar aside.

Measure your cookie dough into 1-tablespoon (25-g) balls, rolling and packing the dough with the palm of your hands. Roll the balls in the bowl of cinnamon sugar and place them 2 inches (5 cm) apart on the prepared baking sheets. Indent the center of each cookie with your thumb or the back of a ¼-teaspoon measuring spoon. Place the baking sheets in the fridge to chill the dough for 15 minutes. Remove the baking sheets from the fridge, and then fill each cookie with some of the blackberry jam.

Bake the cookies on the oven's middle rack for 14 to 15 minutes, until they are slightly golden. Place the baking sheets on a wire rack for 5 minutes. Then gently transfer the cookies to the rack to completely cool. The jam will set once it's cooled, and you can then stack the cookies to store them in an airtight container. I bet you can't eat just one!

VANILLA-BOURBON MARSHMALLOWS

YIELDS

24 to 36 marshmallows

MARSHMALLOW COATING

1½ cups (180 g) confectioners' sugar

1 cup (128 g) cornstarch

GELATIN BLOOM

½ cup (120 ml) cool water

2 tbsp (24 g) unflavored gelatin powder

MARSHMALLOW SUGAR MIX

1½ cups (300 g) granulated sugar

½ cup (120 ml) water

⅔ cup (160 ml) light corn syrup

2 vanilla beans, scraped

3 tbsp (45 ml) Kentucky bourbon

Homemade marshmallows really do melt in your mouth and make great toppings for pies, cakes, and cookies. And in this recipe, a little bourbon and vanilla add some pizzazz to your hot chocolate or Rice Krispies Treats™. You can make these marshmallows during the winter to share as holiday gifts, or impress your camping friends with a batch to roast after a cookout. They're easier to make than you think—and once you have tasted a homemade marshmallow, store-bought marshmallows just can't compare.

To make the marshmallow coating, whisk together the confectioners' sugar and cornstarch in a large bowl.

Lightly spray an 8 x 8–inch (20 x 20–cm) baking pan with nonstick baking spray. Line the pan with parchment paper, making sure that the parchment paper hangs over all four sides of the pan but lies flat in the pan's bottom. Sift a thick layer of the marshmallow coating over the bottom and sides of the baking pan. Set the remaining marshmallow coating aside for later.

Next, make the gelatin bloom by stirring together the water and gelatin in the bowl of a stand mixer fitted with the whisk attachment. Allow the mixture to rest for 10 to 15 minutes, until it has bloomed, or thickened.

Meanwhile, make the marshmallow sugar mix. In a medium saucepan, combine the granulated sugar, water, and corn syrup. Cook the mixture over low heat for 2 to 3 minutes, until the sugar has dissolved.

Increase the heat to medium-high, bring the mixture to a boil, and cook it for 6 to 7 minutes, until its temperature reads 240°F (115°C) on a candy thermometer, which is the soft-ball stage. Remove the saucepan from the stove.

With the stand mixer running at medium-high speed, very carefully and slowly pour the hot sugar syrup into the gelatin mixture. Aim for the area between the whisk and the side of the bowl.

Add the vanilla bean seeds and increase the mixer's speed to high. Whip the mixture for 8 to 10 minutes, until the mixture has tripled in size. It should be very thick and fluffy.

(CONTINUED)

Vanilla-Bourbon Marshmallows (Continued)

Pour in the bourbon and gently fold it into the marshmallow cream with a rubber spatula. Spoon the marshmallow cream into the prepared baking pan with a rubber spatula and level its surface with the spatula. Generously sift the marshmallow coating over the top to create a thick blanket on the marshmallow cream.

Let the marshmallow sit, uncovered, in a cool, dry place for 4 hours, or overnight, to dry out and firm up.

Using the overhanging parchment paper, lift the marshmallow square from the pan and place the whole marshmallow on a cutting board. Dust a sharp knife with confectioners' sugar and cut the marshmallow into squares. Coat the marshmallows with more of the marshmallow coating, dipping the sides of the marshmallows in the coating if you like. Serve the marshmallows with your favorite hot drink, cookies, cake, or pie, or just eat them plain! Store the marshmallows in an airtight container for up to 1 week.

MOM'S PERSIMMON PUDDING BARS

YIELDS
30 to 40 servings

PERSIMMON PUDDING
4 lbs (1.8 kg) wild persimmons (see Note)

3 cups (375 g) all-purpose flour

2 tsp (10 g) baking powder

1 tsp kosher salt

1 tsp ground cinnamon

½ tsp ground nutmeg

½ tsp ground cloves

2½ cups (500 g) sugar

2½ cups (600 ml) whole milk, at room temperature

4 large eggs, lightly beaten

½ cup (114 g) unsalted butter, melted and slightly cooled

BOTTOM CRUST
2 cups (256 g) finely chopped pitted Medjool dates

2 cups (256 g) finely chopped dried figs

1 cup (84 g) sweetened shredded coconut

1 cup (224 g) coconut oil, melted and slightly cooled

2 tbsp (30 ml) pure vanilla extract

2 tbsp (30 ml) maple syrup

3 cups (375 g) all-purpose flour

There's a wild persimmon tree that grows next to my parents' home in North Carolina. It's a treasured ornamental fruit tree that my mom harvests in the late fall to make her famous persimmon pudding. This pumpkin pie–textured treat has been passed down from my great-grandmother to my grandmother, from my grandmother to my mom, and now to me. I've added a bottom crust made with coconut and dried fruit to this labor-of-love dessert that I hope you will enjoy as much as we do.

Prepare the persimmon pulp for the persimmon pudding first. Ripe wild persimmons are deep apricot and purple in color with pink highlights. After you gather the persimmons, you must wash each one and remove the caps. Be sure to smell them; if they have a sour smell, they are spoiled. Throw any sour persimmons away. Do not use persimmons that are not completely ripe either, because they will pucker your mouth and ruin the entire pudding. It only takes one bad persimmon to spoil the pudding.

After washing the persimmons, place them in a colander set inside a large bowl. Using the back of a large metal spoon, mash the persimmons through the colander into the bowl to make the pulp. Be careful not to scrape any of the black coating from the seeds and to avoid getting any seeds in the pulp, since they are bitter and will ruin the flavor of your pudding. Be careful to keep the skins separate from the pulp as well. Place the pulp in a large bowl, ensuring you have 4 cups (976 g) of pulp, and set the bowl aside.

Next, make the bottom crust for your pudding. Spray two 9 x 12 x 2–inch (23 x 30 x 5–cm) metal baking pans with nonstick baking spray. Line the bottom of the pans with parchment paper, making sure that it hangs over the long sides of the pans. Note that the ingredients for the crust will make a double batch of crust to be divided between the two baking pans.

Place the dates, figs, shredded coconut, oil, vanilla, maple syrup, and flour in a large bowl and mix well to combine the ingredients. Press the crust mixture into the bottoms of the prepared baking pans with your fingers to create an even layer in each pan.

(CONTINUED)

Mom's Persimmon Pudding Bars (Continued)

Preheat the oven to 350°F (180°C).

Continue preparing the persimmon pudding. In a small bowl, whisk together the flour, baking powder, salt, cinnamon, nutmeg, and cloves. In a large bowl, use a handheld mixer to beat together the persimmon pulp, sugar, milk, and eggs. Add the flour mixture and mix everything well. Add the butter and mix the ingredients well. Divide the pudding evenly between the two crusts. Bang each baking pan gently on the counter to make sure any air bubbles rise to the top of the pudding.

Place the baking pans on the oven's middle rack. Bake the pudding bars for 50 to 60 minutes, or until they are firm and lightly browned. Place the baking pans on a wire rack and let the pudding bars cool completely. Cover the baking pans with aluminum foil and refrigerate the pudding bars for 1 hour, or until you are ready to serve them. Cut the pudding bars into squares and serve them.

NOTE

Use Fuyu persimmons if wild persimmons are unavailable. This variety is best when ripe, firm, and sweet inside. Freeze any extra pulp in an airtight container to have it on hand all year long.

PEANUT BUTTER AND BOURBON S'MORES

YIELDS

20 cookies for making 10 s'mores

SUGAR COATING

¼ cup (50 g) sparkling sugar

2 tbsp (26 g) Black Onyx Chocolate Sugar (see Note)

COOKIES

½ cup (110 g) dark brown sugar

⅓ cup (67 g) granulated sugar

½ tsp baking soda

¼ tsp sea salt

½ tsp ground cinnamon

1 cup (256 g) creamy peanut butter

1 large egg

2 tsp (10 ml) pure vanilla extract

½ cup (85 g) semisweet chocolate chips, roughly chopped

¼ cup (28 g) honey-roasted peanuts, roughly chopped

MARSHMALLOWS

1 recipe Vanilla-Bourbon Marshmallows (page 87), toasted

NOTE

Black Onyx Chocolate Sugar is a brand of chocolate sugar with a brownie-like flavor that can be purchased at spice stores.

Growing up, I enjoyed s'mores made with two graham crackers, a toasted marshmallow, and a piece of dark chocolate. Lots of evenings by the campfire after a fall cookout called for partially burned, gooey-sugar sandwiches. As an adult, I've graduated to peanut butter chocolate chip cookies with bourbon marshmallows. These flourless cookies—coated in sparkling and Black Onyx Chocolate Sugar—create the perfect crunchy vessel for a modern, boozy s'more.

Preheat the oven to 350°F (180°C). Line two rimmed medium baking sheets with parchment paper or silicone baking mats.

To make the sugar coating, stir together the sparkling sugar and Black Onyx Chocolate Sugar in a small bowl. Set the sugar coating aside.

To make the cookies, combine the brown sugar, granulated sugar, baking soda, salt, and cinnamon in the bowl of a stand mixer. Hand-whisk the ingredients to combine them. Add the peanut butter, egg, and vanilla to the bowl. Fit the stand mixer with the paddle attachment, then mix the ingredients at medium speed for a couple of revolutions, until they are well combined. Reduce the mixer's speed to medium-low. Add the chocolate chips and peanuts, mixing to distribute them throughout the cookie dough. Don't overmix the dough.

Using a 1½-tablespoon (23-g) cookie scoop, measure out a dollop of dough. Pack the dough together with your hands, then create a round ball by rolling the dough gently between your palms. Then roll the cookie ball in the sugar coating until it's evenly coated. Transfer the cookie balls to one of the prepared baking sheets, spacing them 1 to 2 inches (2.5 to 5 cm) apart. Using the bottom of a flat glass, press down on the cookie ball gently to flatten it. If the cookie cracks around the edges, reshape it with your fingertips, squeezing it gently to form a round cookie. Repeat with the remainder of the cookie dough.

Bake one baking sheet of cookies at a time on the oven's middle rack for 7 to 8 minutes. The cookies will still be soft and look slightly underdone—don't worry, they will harden as they cool. If you overbake them, they will be too crumbly.

Place the baking sheets on wire racks for 15 minutes. Then gently transfer the cookies to the racks to completely cool. Firm, cooled cookies will be ready to make s'mores.

Take a single cookie and flip it upside down. Place a similarly sized toasted marshmallow on the bottom cookie, then top the marshmallow with another cookie. Alternatively, you can use only one cookie for an open-faced s'more.

CHRISTMAS SUGAR COOKIES

YIELDS
about 24 (4" [10-cm]) cookies

2½ cups (313 g) all-purpose flour

¼ tsp baking soda

¼ tsp baking powder

1 tsp cream of tartar

¼ tsp kosher salt

1 cup (114 g) unsalted butter, cold and cut into cubes

1 cup (200 g) granulated sugar, plus more if needed

1 large egg, lightly beaten

2 tsp (9 g) vanilla bean paste

¾ tsp pure almond extract

Confectioners' sugar, as needed

Sprinkles (optional)

NOTE
You can also decorate any plain cookies with frosting or royal icing after they have cooled.

One thing I look forward to each year is cookie season. Every Christmas Eve that I can remember, I've made cookies with my mom. We make an array of holiday shapes decorated with sprinkles. It's a cherished tradition that I have implemented with my close friends and their children, which means I get to make and eat a ton of sugar cookies! Whether you frost the cookies or add colored crystal decorations, this family-favorite dough with a hint of almond is a tried-and-true winner.

In a medium bowl, stir together the flour, baking soda, baking powder, cream of tartar, and salt.

In the bowl of a stand mixer fitted with a paddle attachment, beat together the butter, granulated sugar, egg, vanilla bean paste, and almond extract at medium speed for 2 to 3 minutes, until the ingredients are smooth. Add the flour mixture and beat the ingredients at low speed for 1 to 2 minutes, until a dough forms. Shape the dough into a flat disk and wrap it tightly in plastic wrap. Refrigerate the cookie dough for a minimum of 2 hours to allow it to rest and firm up.

Preheat the oven to 325°F (165°C). Line two rimmed medium baking sheets with parchment paper.

Remove the chilled cookie dough from the fridge and divide it in half. Wrap one half of the dough in plastic wrap, and store it in the fridge until you are ready to use it.

Dust a work surface with the confectioners' sugar. Roll out one half of the cookie dough until it is ⅛ inch (3 mm) thick. Lightly coat cookie cutters of your choice in confectioners' sugar, then cut out shapes from the dough. Decorate the cookies with additional granulated sugar or sprinkles (if using).

Transfer the cookies to the prepared baking sheets, spacing them 3 inches (8 cm) apart. Keep the cookie dough cold to prevent the cookies from spreading while they bake. I like to place my baking sheet of cookies in the fridge to chill for 10 minutes before baking them.

Bake the cookies on the oven's middle rack for 9 to 11 minutes, rotating the baking sheets halfway through the baking time. The edges of the cookies should begin to turn light gold. Be careful not to overbake the cookies.

Transfer the baking sheets to wire racks to cool for 5 minutes, then gently place the cookies directly on the racks to cool completely.

Repeat with the remaining half of the cookie dough.

GINGERBREAD BROWNIES

YIELDS

9 large brownies

1 cup (125 g) all-purpose flour

⅓ cup (28 g) Dutch-process cocoa powder, sifted

½ tsp baking powder

¼ tsp sea salt

1 tsp ground cinnamon

½ tsp ground ginger

½ tsp ground nutmeg

1 cup (170 g) semisweet chocolate chips

8 tbsp (112 g) unsalted butter, melted

¾ packed cup (165 g) dark brown sugar

¼ cup (50 g) granulated sugar

¼ cup (85 g) unsulfured molasses

2 large eggs

1 large egg yolk

¼ cup (60 ml) neutral oil

3 tbsp (24 g) finely chopped candied ginger

Confectioners' sugar, as needed

These brownies are my version of a single-layer gingerbread cake topped with a dusting of confectioners' sugar. They're a favorite treat that I love to serve throughout the fall and winter with coffee or eggnog. The rich flavor of molasses is even better with chocolate and candied ginger, resulting in a cozy, fudgy brownie. These brownies embody all the warmth of the gingerbread spices with a melt-in-your-mouth texture. Make a batch for a hike to look at the fall leaves or for an on-the-couch afternoon to watch the snow fall.

Preheat the oven to 325°F (165°C). Prepare an 8 x 8–inch (20 x 20–cm) or 9 x 9–inch (23 x 23–cm) baking pan with nonstick baking spray. Line the bottom of the pan with parchment paper, making sure to leave some parchment paper hanging over the sides of the pan for easy removal of the brownies.

In a medium bowl, whisk together the flour, cocoa powder, baking powder, salt, cinnamon, ground ginger, and nutmeg. Set the flour mixture aside.

Place the chocolate chips in a small bowl and pour the warm melted butter over them. Let this mixture sit for about 30 seconds, then stir it with a fork until the chocolate chips are melted and smooth.

In a large bowl, whisk together the brown sugar, granulated sugar, molasses, eggs, egg yolk, and oil until the ingredients are smooth. Add the melted chocolate and stir the mixture again until everything is combined.

Spoon half of the flour mixture into the sugar-molasses mixture, slowly mixing the two with a rubber spatula in a figure-eight pattern and scraping around the sides of the bowl a couple of times, until there are no more flour streaks. Repeat this process with the remaining half of the flour mixture. Be gentle when mixing and avoid vigorous stirring.

Fold in the candied ginger until it is just distributed throughout the brownie batter. Transfer the thick brownie batter into the prepared baking pan. Using an offset spatula, level the batter as best you can.

Place the baking pan on the oven's middle rack and bake the brownies for 25 to 30 minutes, until the sides are pulling away from the pan and a crinkled crust appears on the top. A toothpick inserted into the center may come out with a few gooey crumbs, but that's just fine. The brownies will continue to firm up as they cool. Don't overbake them, or you'll have a big dry square when it cools. Remember, when you are using real chocolate, it gets thin when it melts and firms as it cools.

Place the baking pan on a wire rack to allow the brownies to completely cool. Grab the overhanging pieces of parchment paper and lift the brownie square from the pan and transfer it to a cutting board. Take a large, sharp, smooth knife and slice the brownie into individual squares. Dust the brownies lightly with the confectioners' sugar before devouring them.

CHOCOLATE-CHAI WHOOPIE PIES

YIELDS

6 whoopie pies

COOKIES

2 cups (250 g) all-purpose flour

¼ cup (32 g) rye flour

½ cup (43 g) Dutch-process cocoa powder, sifted

1 tsp baking powder

½ tsp baking soda

½ tsp kosher salt

2 tsp (10 g) espresso powder

1 tsp chai spice

½ cup (114 g) unsalted butter, at room temperature

1 packed cup (220 g) dark brown sugar

1 large egg, at room temperature

2 tsp (10 ml) pure vanilla extract

¾ cup (180 ml) full-fat buttermilk, well shaken and at room temperature

2 tbsp (30 ml) brewed coffee, slightly warm

Turbinado sugar, as needed

MARSHMALLOW CHAI FILLING

½ cup (114 g) unsalted butter

1½ cups (180 g) confectioners' sugar

1 tbsp (6 g) chai spice

¼ tsp sea salt

1½ cups (188 g) marshmallow creme

1 tsp pure vanilla extract

Whoopie pies are a familiar item at fairground vendors, country stores, and small bakeries. Is it a cookie, pie, or cake sandwich? I've always thought of them as jumbo versions of the Oreo cookie. They are the perfect sweet tooth indulgence. Filled with fluffy marshmallow cream, these classic southern bake-sale treats reflect my love for chocolate-chai lattes.

Preheat the oven to 350°F (180°C). Line two rimmed large baking sheets with parchment paper or silicone baking mats.

Make the cookies first. In a medium bowl, whisk together the all-purpose flour, rye flour, cocoa powder, baking powder, baking soda, salt, espresso powder, and chai spice. Set the flour mixture aside.

In the bowl of a stand mixer fitted with the paddle attachment, beat together the butter and brown sugar at medium speed for 2 to 3 minutes, until the mixture forms a paste. Add the egg and vanilla and mix again to combine the ingredients. Scrape the bottom and sides of the bowl with a rubber spatula as needed to make sure all of the ingredients are incorporated. With the mixer running at medium-low speed, spoon in one-third of the flour mixture, alternating it with ¼ cup (60 ml) of the buttermilk. Add another one-third of the flour mixture, another ¼ cup (60 ml) of the buttermilk, the remaining one-third of the flour mixture, and the remaining ¼ cup (60 ml) of the buttermilk. Finally, pour in the warm coffee and mix the ingredients for 2 to 3 minutes, until a thick cake batter forms. Measure ¼ cup (60 g) of the batter and drop it onto the prepared baking sheets, spacing the dollops 2 inches (5 cm) apart. Sprinkle the dollops with the turbinado sugar.

Place one baking sheet on the oven's middle rack and bake the cookies for 15 to 18 minutes, until they are puffy and a toothpick inserted into the center comes out clean. Remove the baking sheet from the oven and carefully transfer the warm cookies to a wire rack using a rubber spatula. Repeat this process with the second baking sheet of cookies. Allow the cookies to cool completely before assembling the whoopie pies.

While the cookies are cooling, prepare the marshmallow chai filling. In a large bowl, use a handheld mixer to beat the butter at medium speed for 2 to 3 minutes, until it is smooth. Reduce the mixer's speed to low and add the confectioners' sugar, chai spice, and salt. Add the marshmallow creme and vanilla. Increase the mixer's speed to medium and mix the ingredients for 1 to 2 minutes, until they are smooth. Transfer the marshmallow chai filling to a large piping bag.

To assemble the whoopie pies, place one cookie, domed side down, on a plate. Pipe the flat side with the marshmallow chai filling. Place the flat side of another cookie on the marshmallow chai filling to make a sandwich. Wrap the individual whoopie pies in plastic wrap until you are ready to eat them.

HONEY-ROASTED PEANUT BUTTER FUDGE

FUDGE

8 tbsp (112 g) unsalted butter

2 cups (440 g) light brown sugar

½ cup (120 ml) heavy cream

2 tsp (10 ml) pure vanilla extract

1 cup (256 g) creamy peanut butter

2 tbsp (42 g) whipped honey

3½ cups (420 g) confectioners' sugar

1 cup (113 g) roughly chopped honey-roasted peanuts

CHOCOLATE TOPPING

1 cup (170 g) roughly chopped dark chocolate, melted

¼ cup (28 g) roughly chopped honey-roasted peanuts

NOTE

Whipped or creamed honey can be purchased at all grocery stores. It's thicker than regular honey, so it helps form a paste. Using regular honey in this recipe will result in a runny fudge.

My mom makes several batches of peanut butter fudge every Christmas, lovingly placing slices in holiday-themed canisters tied with ribbon for gifting. Fudge is a classic holiday dessert that is a tradition in my house too. This peanut butter fudge recipe has a great sweet-and-salty flavor, with bits of honey-roasted peanuts and a rich chocolate topping. All the texture boxes are ticked with chewy, creamy, crunchy elements. Add a little flaky sea salt on top if you're feeling adventurous. Warning: This fudge is highly addictive, and you may need a second batch just in case.

Prepare an 8 x 8–inch (20 x 20–cm), 9 x 9–inch (23 x 23–cm), or 7 x 11–inch (18 x 28–cm) baking pan with a light coating of nonstick baking spray. Line the bottom of the baking pan with a sheet of parchment paper that is long enough to hang over two sides of the pan. Once the fudge is set, you can grab the overhanging pieces of parchment paper and lift the fudge from the baking pan for easy slicing.

To make the fudge, place the butter, brown sugar, heavy cream, and vanilla in a medium saucepan over medium-high heat. Stir the mixture occasionally with a wooden spoon until the sugar and butter are melted. Cook the mixture for 2 to 3 minutes, until you start to see bubbles in the center, but don't let it come to a full boil. Add the peanut butter and whipped honey, and stir the ingredients until the mixture is smooth. Remove the saucepan from the heat.

Place the confectioners' sugar in the bowl of a stand mixer fitted with a paddle attachment and carefully pour the warm peanut butter mixture on top of the confectioners' sugar.

Start mixing the ingredients at medium-low speed and gradually sprinkle in the peanuts as you increase the speed to medium-high. Mix the ingredients for about 2 minutes, until the mixture resembles the consistency of a thick cookie dough.

Transfer the fudge to the prepared baking pan and level it using your fingertips or a small rubber spatula.

Next, make the chocolate topping. Pour the melted chocolate over the fudge and level it with an offset spatula. Allow the chocolate to cool for about 5 minutes, then sprinkle it with the peanuts. Allow the chocolate to sit and firm up for a minimum of 1 hour before slicing the fudge. Once the fudge has set, it can be stored at room temperature.

Labor-of-Love Breads

Fill my kitchen with the smell of warm bread!

No matter where I find myself in the South, two things remain constant: A banana bread loaf is the perfect gift for any occasion, and rolls must accompany every dinner meal.

I'm sharing some recipes for yeast and quick breads in this chapter to satisfy your breakfast, dinner, and dessert needs. Dip Country Ham Fantails (page 117) in sunny-side-up eggs, and try a warm slice of Mountain Molasses Cornbread (page 111) with whipped orange butter. Make a little French toast with my Cinnamon Raisin Bread (page 107) or a fully loaded burger with some Backyard Burger Buns (page 115).

Whether you choose to slather butter, molasses, honey, or icing on your warm bread, I know it will be delicious!

TIPS FOR SUCCESS

- For yeast breads, make sure the yeast is fresh and not out of date. Check the temperature of the milk or water before adding it to the yeast. Liquid that is too warm will kill the yeast and prevent your bread from rising.

- Check the gluten formation in a yeast dough by tearing off a small piece and stretching it with your fingertips. If you can see through it like a windowpane without it breaking, the dough is ready.

- Place covered yeast dough in a cold oven with the light on for a warm rising location.

- When making loaves of quick bread, line the baking pan with overhanging parchment paper so you can easily lift out the baked bread.

- Wrap unfrosted quick breads in plastic wrap and store them at room temperature for 2 to 3 days. Place yeast breads in a closed paper bag and store them at room temperature for 3 to 4 days.

ROASTED SWEET POTATO BREAD

YIELDS

1 (9 x 5" [23 x 13-cm]) loaf

CANDIED WALNUTS

2 cups (228 g) walnut halves

½ cup (100 g) granulated sugar

2 tbsp (28 g) unsalted butter

BREAD

¼ cup (56 g) unsalted butter

2 sweet potatoes (see Note)

2 cups (250 g) cake flour

½ tsp baking powder

1 tsp baking soda

½ tsp kosher salt

2 tsp (4 g) ground cinnamon

1 tsp ground nutmeg

½ tsp ground ginger

¼ tsp ground cloves

¼ tsp ground allspice

¼ tsp ground cardamom

1¼ cups (275 g) light brown sugar

2 large eggs

¼ cup (60 ml) apple butter

2 tsp (10 ml) pure vanilla extract

MAPLE-VANILLA GLAZE

1 cup (120 g) confectioners' sugar, plus more if needed

1 tbsp (15 ml) whole milk, plus more if needed

2 tsp (10 ml) pure vanilla extract

1 tsp pure maple syrup

⅛ tsp kosher salt

Sweet potatoes are a staple ingredient in just about every southern kitchen and restaurant. These sweet little spuds are mixed into casseroles, pies, or breads that are served throughout the year, but they are enjoyed the most during the fall and holiday seasons. My favorite Thanksgiving side is a roasted sweet potato covered in butter and sprinkled with brown sugar and cinnamon. I wanted to transform that flavor into a dessert bread that I could enjoy with coffee or as an after-dinner delight. Rich brown butter and roasted sweet potato puree make this the perfect autumn treat. The spiced bread is complemented by a sweet vanilla glaze and topped with crunchy candied walnuts.

This recipe has a few texture layers, each one important to creating an amazing flavor and texture profile. I recommend making the candied walnuts at least 1 hour before making the rest of the recipe. Line a flat large baking sheet with a silicone baking mat. Set the baking sheet aside. Place the walnuts, granulated sugar, and butter in a medium skillet over medium heat. As the butter melts and the sugar turns to liquid, stir the mixture for 2 to 3 minutes with a heatproof rubber spatula to coat the walnuts evenly. Quickly transfer the nuts to the prepared baking sheet and spread them apart to prevent them from clumping together. A candy crust will form on the walnuts as they cool to room temperature. If you make the walnuts more than 1 hour ahead of making the remainder of this recipe, store them in an airtight container until you are ready to use them.

Now, move on to preparing your bread. Make the brown butter by melting the butter in a light-colored medium skillet over medium heat. A white foam will form on the butter, and it will start to crackle and pop. Cook the butter for 5 to 7 minutes, stirring it gently, until it is amber brown in color and releasing a nutty fragrance. The milk solids at the bottom of the skillet will look like small dark brown dots, and they are full of flavor. Pour the browned butter into a heatproof small bowl. Set the browned butter aside to cool down to room temperature before using it.

(CONTINUED)

ROASTED SWEET POTATO BREAD (CONTINUED)

Roasting the sweet potatoes will add a nice caramelized flavor to the puree. Preheat the oven to 400°F (200°C). Pierce the sweet potatoes several times with a fork and place them on a medium baking sheet. Bake the sweet potatoes for about 45 minutes, until they are fork-tender. Let the sweet potatoes cool to room temperature before scooping out the flesh. Transfer the roasted sweet potato flesh to a food processor, add the browned butter, and process until the mixture is smooth. Measure 1½ cups (366 g) of the puree and set it aside.

Reduce the oven temperature to 350°F (180°C). Prepare a 9 x 5–inch (23 x 13–cm) loaf pan with a thin coating of nonstick baking spray. Line the bottom of the pan with parchment paper, making sure that the parchment paper hangs over the long sides of the pan for easy removal after the bread is baked.

In a medium bowl, whisk together the flour, baking powder, baking soda, salt, cinnamon, nutmeg, ginger, cloves, allspice, and cardamom. Set the flour mixture aside.

In a large bowl, whisk together the brown sugar, eggs, roasted sweet potato puree, apple butter, and vanilla until the mixture is smooth.

Using a rubber spatula, fold one-third of the flour mixture into the potato mixture until you no longer see streaks of flour. Repeat this process with the remaining flour mixture, one-third at a time. Avoid overmixing the ingredients, which will create a dense bread.

Transfer the batter to the prepared loaf pan. Bake the bread in the center of the oven's middle rack for 50 to 60 minutes, or until a toothpick inserted into the center comes out with just a few crumbs. Remove the loaf pan from the oven and place it on a wire rack to completely cool.

To make the maple-vanilla glaze, combine the confectioners' sugar, milk, vanilla, maple syrup, and salt in a medium bowl. Whisk the ingredients until they are smooth. To thicken the glaze, whisk in additional confectioners' sugar, 1 tablespoon (8 g) at a time. To make the glaze thinner, add an additional 1 teaspoon of milk and whisk the glaze again.

Assemble the sweet potato bread by grabbing the overhanging parchment paper and lifting the cooled bread out of the loaf pan and placing the bread on a serving dish. Pour the maple-vanilla glaze over the loaf and then top it with the candied walnuts. Slice and serve the bread.

NOTE

Use fresh sweet potatoes that have red or orange skin with rich orange flesh on the inside for this bread recipe. My favorites to use are Red Garnet and Jewel.

CINNAMON RAISIN BREAD

YIELDS

1 (9 x 5" [23 x 13–cm]) loaf

DOUGH

2¼ tsp (7 g) active dry yeast

1 cup (240 ml) whole milk, warmed to 105 to 110°F (40 to 45°C), divided

¼ cup (55 g) light brown sugar

2 large eggs

5 tbsp (70 g) unsalted butter, melted and slightly cooled

3½ cups (438 g) plus 1 tbsp (8 g) all-purpose flour, plus more as needed

1 tsp kosher salt

1 tsp ground cinnamon

½ cup (64 g) raisins

FILLING

2 tbsp (28 g) dark brown sugar

¼ cup (50 g) granulated sugar

2 tbsp (12 g) ground cinnamon

1 tbsp (8 g) all-purpose flour

⅛ tsp sea salt

EGG WASH

1 large egg

1 tsp water

TOPPING

2 tbsp (26 g) granulated sugar

¼ tsp ground cinnamon

My favorite way to enjoy toast is with my mom's homemade cinnamon raisin bread. When she makes bread, there is always one plain loaf and one cinnamon raisin loaf cooling on the counter. I love slices of cinnamon raisin bread smothered with jam and honey butter or transformed into French toast. My version has dark brown sugar in the filling and a coating of cinnamon sugar on top. This bread is irresistible fresh and warm from the oven.

To make the dough, the first step is to activate the yeast. Place the yeast, ½ cup (120 ml) of the milk, and the light brown sugar in the bowl of a stand mixer fitted with the dough hook attachment and gently stir the ingredients together. Let the mixture rest for 10 minutes, until it is frothy. Pour in the remaining ½ cup (120 ml) of milk, the eggs, and butter. With the mixer running at medium-low speed, start to mix the ingredients. Stop the mixer once the ingredients are combined.

In a medium bowl, whisk together the flour, salt, and cinnamon. Slowly add the flour mixture to the milk mixture while mixing the ingredients at medium-low speed. Once all of the flour mixture is added, continue to mix the dough for about 3 minutes, until it has a shaggy texture. Add the raisins and mix the ingredients again for about 7 minutes. The dough will be smooth, sticky, and clinging to the sides of the bowl. Cover the bowl with plastic wrap and place it in a warm, draft-free location to allow the dough to rise for 1 to 2 hours, until the dough has doubled in size.

Prepare a 9 x 5–inch (23 x 13–cm) loaf pan by greasing it with butter or a light coating of nonstick baking spray. Line the loaf pan with parchment paper, ensuring that the parchment paper hangs over the sides of the pan.

Once the dough has doubled in size, lightly dust a work surface with flour. Then lightly coat the top of your hand with flour and press your fist down into the dough to release excess air. Scrape the dough out of the bowl with your hand and place it on the prepared work surface. Using a floured rolling pin, roll out the dough to a 14 x 8–inch (36 x 20–cm) rectangle.

(CONTINUED)

Cinnamon Raisin Bread (Continued)

Now it's time to make the filling. In a small bowl, whisk together the dark brown sugar, granulated sugar, cinnamon, flour, and salt.

Make the egg wash. In a small bowl, use a fork to beat together the egg and water.

Brush the egg wash across the dough, leaving a 1-inch (2.5-cm) border exposed. Sprinkle the filling over the egg wash in an even layer. Roll the rectangle of dough, starting at the short side, into a tight log. Tuck the ends underneath the dough, then carefully lift the dough and place it into the prepared loaf pan, seam side down. Loosely cover the dough with a tea towel and allow it to rest for 45 to 60 minutes, until it has puffed up just a bit over the top of the pan.

Preheat the oven to 400°F (200°C).

While the oven is preheating, make the topping. In a small bowl, stir together the granulated sugar and cinnamon with a fork. Remove the towel from the dough and gently brush it with the egg wash. Sprinkle the topping generously across the top of the loaf.

Place the loaf pan on the oven's middle rack and bake the bread for 10 minutes. Reduce the oven's temperature to 350°F (180°C) and bake the bread for 25 to 30 minutes, until the bread's internal temperature has reached 190°F (90°C) and the loaf sounds hollow when it is tapped. Place the loaf pan on a wire rack for 15 minutes, then lift or shake the loaf from the pan. Set the loaf directly on the rack to cool for 15 minutes, then slice it and serve it warm.

MOUNTAIN MOLASSES CORNBREAD

CORNBREAD

1 cup (125 g) plus 2 tbsp (16 g) all-purpose flour, divided

¾ cup (94 g) whole-wheat flour

¾ cup (113 g) yellow cornmeal

⅓ cup (67 g) granulated sugar

2 tsp (10 g) baking powder

½ tsp baking soda

½ tsp kosher salt

1¼ cups (300 ml) full-fat buttermilk

⅓ cup (113 g) unsulfured light or dark molasses (not blackstrap)

1 large egg, lightly beaten

3 tbsp (42 g) unsalted butter, melted and cooled

1 cup (164 g) fresh or drained canned yellow corn kernels

ORANGE BUTTER

½ cup (114 g) unsalted butter, softened

2 tbsp (12 g) fresh orange zest

2 tbsp (16 g) confectioners' sugar

It's true: I'm a huge honey fan. For many years, I only used molasses when I made gingerbread cookies. But when I lived in the Appalachian Mountains, I was introduced to mixing butter and molasses together and spreading it onto cornbread. The combination results in a delightful flavor that works well in a cornbread loaf smeared with my grandmother's whipped orange butter.

Preheat the oven to 400°F (200°C). Lightly coat an 11 x 7 x 1½–inch (28 x 18 x 4–cm) or 8 x 8–inch (20 x 20–cm) metal baking pan with nonstick baking spray.

To make the cornbread, whisk together 1 cup (125 g) of the all-purpose flour, the whole-wheat flour, cornmeal, granulated sugar, baking powder, baking soda, and salt in a large bowl.

In a medium bowl, stir together the buttermilk, molasses, egg, and butter. Pour the milk mixture into the flour mixture and stir until the two are just combined. Don't overmix the batter.

In a small bowl, stir together the corn kernels and the remaining 2 tablespoons (16 g) of all-purpose flour until the corn is evenly coated. This helps prevent the corn from sinking to the bottom of your loaf. Fold the corn into the batter, then transfer the batter to the prepared baking pan.

Bake the cornbread on the oven's middle rack for 20 to 25 minutes, until a toothpick inserted into the center comes out clean. Place the baking pan on a wire rack to cool for 10 minutes.

While the cornbread is cooling, make the orange butter. In a medium bowl, use a handheld mixer to whip together the butter, orange zest, and confectioners' sugar at medium speed for 1 to 2 minutes, until the mixture is fluffy. Scrape the sides and bottom of the bowl with a spatula to make sure everything is well mixed.

Slather a generous amount of the orange butter onto a slice of the warm cornbread.

CHEESY DILLY DINNER ROLLS

YIELDS

12 dinner rolls

ROLLS

1 cup (240 ml) whole milk, warmed to 105 to 110°F (40 to 45°C)

2 tbsp (30 ml) clover honey

2¼ tsp (7 g) active dry yeast

3 cups (375 g) all-purpose flour, plus more as needed

1 tsp kosher salt

1 tbsp (6 g) minced fresh dill

1 large egg, lightly beaten

5 tbsp (70 g) unsalted butter, melted and cooled, plus more as needed

1½ cups (120 g) grated Havarti cheese with dill

TOPPING

4 tbsp (56 g) unsalted butter, melted, divided

Dinner at my grandmother's house always included fresh homemade rolls. Golden, soft, and buttery with the occasional topping of cheese—a little effort goes a long way. These dilly rolls are a step up from traditional plain rolls, incorporating fresh dill from the garden and warm Havarti cheese. They're the perfect vessel for sopping up chili, soup, or spaghetti sauce.

To make the rolls, first activate the yeast. In the bowl of a stand mixer fitted with the dough hook attachment, stir together the milk, honey, and yeast. Let the mixture sit for about 10 minutes, until it is foamy.

Meanwhile, in a medium bowl, whisk together the flour, salt, and dill. Once the yeast mixture is frothy, add the egg and butter. With the mixer running at medium-low speed, slowly spoon the flour mixture into the yeast mixture. After all the flour has been added, increase the mixer's speed to medium-high and beat the dough for 4 to 5 minutes. It should pull away from the sides of the bowl while still sticking to the very bottom, and it should almost resemble a tornado while you are mixing. It should be smooth and slightly tacky but not sticky.

Lightly grease a large bowl with butter. Transfer the dough to the prepared bowl, then cover it with plastic wrap. Set the bowl in a warm, draft-free location to allow the dough to rise for 1 to 2 hours, until it has doubled in size. Lightly dust a work surface with flour. Then lightly coat the top of your hand with flour. Slowly punch down the dough with your fist to release any excess air. Transfer the dough to the prepared surface and, using a pastry scraper, divide the dough into 12 equal pieces. If you have a kitchen scale, it is a great tool for weighing and equally dividing dough.

Cupping your hand over a piece of dough on the work surface, lightly use your palm to roll the dough into a ball. The dough should somewhat grip the work surface. Flatten the ball gently with your hand into a rough square. Place 2 tablespoons (10 g) of the Havarti cheese in the center of the dough square. Bring each corner of the dough over the cheese to enclose it in the dough. Place the dough seam side down on the work surface and reroll it into a ball. Repeat this process with the remaining dough and Havarti cheese.

Preheat the oven to 375°F (190°C). Line a large baking pan with parchment paper. Place the dough balls in the prepared baking pan. Top the rolls by brushing them with 2 tablespoons (30 ml) of the butter, then loosely cover the rolls with a light tea towel. Place the rolls in a warm, draft-free location to rise for 30 to 45 minutes, until they have puffed up. Transfer the baking pan to the oven's middle rack and bake the rolls for 20 to 25 minutes, until they have risen and their tops are slightly golden. Remove the pan from the oven and brush the warm rolls with the remaining 2 tablespoons (30 ml) of butter. Let the rolls cool slightly before serving them.

BACKYARD BURGER BUNS

YIELDS

12 large burger buns

BUNS

½ sweet potato

2½ cups (313 g) all-purpose flour, plus more as needed

2 cups (250 g) bread flour

2 tsp (6 g) sea salt

8 tbsp (112 g) unsalted butter, at room temperature, divided

1 cup (52 g) diced yellow onion

2½ tsp (8 g) active dry yeast

¾ cup (180 ml) water, warmed to 105 to 110°F (40 to 45°C)

2 tbsp (30 ml) sourwood honey

2 large eggs, lightly beaten

TOPPING

2 tsp (6 g) sea salt

1 tsp poppy seeds

1 tsp chia seeds

1 tbsp (9 g) sesame seeds

½ tsp onion powder

EGG WASH

1 large egg

1 tsp water

Nothing screams summer evenings more than the smell of burgers on the grill. I love a good beef burger covered in cheese and barbecue sauce inside a homemade bun. Fluffy onion sweet potato buns topped with seeds are perfect for burgers, chicken salad, pulled pork, or bacon, egg, and cheese breakfast melts. Skip the squished store-bought buns and mix up a batch of these jumbo buns for your next cookout.

To make the buns, preheat the oven to 425°F (220°C). Line a small baking sheet with parchment paper. Pierce the sweet potato a few times with a fork and place it on the prepared baking sheet. Bake the sweet potato for 20 minutes, until it is fork-tender. Let it cool enough to handle, and then scrape out the flesh. Transfer the sweet potato flesh to a blender and blend until it is smooth. Measure ½ cup (122 g) of the sweet potato puree, then set the puree aside.

Next, whisk together the all-purpose flour, bread flour, and salt in a medium bowl. Set the flour mixture aside.

In a medium skillet over medium heat, melt 2 tablespoons (28 g) of the butter. Add the onion and sauté it for 20 minutes, or until it has become a caramel color. Remove the skillet from the heat and allow the onion to cool to room temperature.

Prepare your dough by first stirring together the yeast, water, and honey in the bowl of a stand mixer fitted with the paddle attachment. Let the yeast mixture sit for about 10 minutes, until it is foamy.

While the yeast mixture is resting, lightly grease a large bowl with oil. Set the bowl aside.

Add the remaining 6 tablespoons (84 g) of butter, the eggs, sweet potato puree, and sautéed onion. Mix the ingredients together at medium speed until they are combined.

Fit the stand mixer with the dough hook attachment and slowly spoon in the flour mixture while mixing the ingredients at medium-low speed. Once all of the flour is added, increase the mixer's speed to medium-high and beat the dough for 6 to 8 minutes, until a smooth, elastic dough forms and pulls away from the sides of the bowl. Transfer the dough to the prepared bowl. Place the bowl in a warm, draft-free location to allow the dough to rise for 1 to 2 hours, or until it has doubled in size.

(CONTINUED)

BACKYARD BURGER BUNS (CONTINUED)

Line a rimmed large baking sheet with parchment paper. Lightly dust a work surface with flour. Then lightly coat the top of your hand with flour. Gently press down on the dough with your floured fist to release any excess air. Weigh the dough and divide it into 12 equal pieces. Cup the palm of your hand over a piece of dough and lightly roll it in a circular motion on the prepared work surface to create a smooth ball. Repeat this process with the remaining dough. Place the buns on the prepared baking sheet. Loosely cover the buns with a light tea towel and allow them to rise in a warm, draft-free area for 30 minutes, or until they have doubled in size.

Meanwhile, make the topping. In a small bowl, stir together the salt, poppy seeds, chia seeds, sesame seeds, and onion powder. Set the topping aside.

Preheat the oven to 350°F (180°C). While the oven is preheating, make the egg wash. In a small bowl, use a fork to stir together the egg and water. Very gently brush each bun with the egg wash, and then sprinkle the buns with the topping.

Bake the buns on the oven's middle rack for 28 to 30 minutes, or until they are golden brown. Transfer the baking sheet to a wire rack to cool for 5 minutes, then transfer the buns to the rack to completely cool.

COUNTRY HAM FANTAILS WITH REDEYE GRAVY

YIELDS

8 fantail biscuits

FANTAILS

12 oz (336 g) center-cut country ham

3 cups (375 g) all-purpose flour, plus more as needed

¼ tsp sea salt

2¼ tsp (7 g) active dry yeast

¼ cup (60 ml) water, warmed to 105 to 110°F (40 to 45°C)

2 tbsp (30 ml) sourwood honey

¾ cup (180 ml) full-fat buttermilk, well shaken and at room temperature

8 tbsp (112 g) unsalted butter, melted and cooled, divided

Oil, as needed

2 tbsp (30 ml) Dijon mustard, plus more if needed

12 oz (336 g) Swiss cheese, sliced into 2" (5-cm) squares, plus more if needed

TOPPING

1 tbsp (9 g) poppy seeds

2 tbsp (28 g) unsalted butter, melted

REDEYE GRAVY

½ cup (120 ml) strong brewed black coffee

1 tbsp (14 g) unsalted butter

1 packed tsp dark brown sugar

Two things you need to try in the South for breakfast are country ham biscuits and redeye gravy, a country-café menu item that I've requested since my first encounter. Coffee mixed with pork grease makes a delicious, hot gravy. This recipe is an amalgamation of my grandmother's ham and Swiss poppy seed sliders and my love for country ham, resulting in a fun fantail biscuit. Add as much or as little gravy as you like, and maybe pair the dish with some sunny-side-up eggs while you're at it!

To make the fantails, cook the country ham. Place the country ham in a medium skillet over medium-high heat and cook it in its own fat for about 10 minutes, flipping it every 2 minutes, until it is golden brown on both sides. Transfer the ham to a plate lined with paper towels to drain the excess grease, but do not drain the skillet. Set aside the skillet with the reserved grease. Let the ham cool completely, then slice the ham into 2-inch (5-cm) squares.

In a medium bowl, whisk together the flour and salt. Set the flour mixture aside.

In the bowl of a stand mixer fitted with the dough hook attachment, stir together the yeast, water, and honey. Let the yeast mixture sit for 5 to 10 minutes, until it is foamy. Add the buttermilk and 6 tablespoons (90 ml) of the butter to the yeast mixture and mix the ingredients at medium speed for 30 to 60 seconds. While the mixer is running, slowly spoon in the flour mixture. Once all the flour is incorporated, increase the mixer's speed to medium-high and mix the dough for 5 to 6 minutes, until a smooth dough forms and pulls away from the sides of the bowl.

Lightly grease a large bowl with oil. Transfer the dough to the prepared bowl and cover the bowl with plastic wrap. Set the bowl in a warm, draft-free place to allow the dough to rise for 1 to 2 hours, until it has doubled in size.

Prepare an 8- or 12-cavity muffin pan with nonstick baking spray. Set the muffin pan aside. Remove the plastic wrap from the bowl. Lightly dust a work surface with flour. Then lightly coat the top of your hand with flour. Gently press your floured fist down into the dough, releasing any excess air. Transfer the dough to the prepared work surface and divide it into two equal pieces. Weigh the dough for the best results.

(CONTINUED)

COUNTRY HAM FANTAILS WITH REDEYE GRAVY (CONTINUED)

Take one half of the dough and roll it into a 12 x 12–inch (30 x 30–cm) square. Using a pastry scraper or sharp knife, cut the dough into four even strips, then cut the strips into four equal pieces, for a total of 16 small pieces. You will use four even squares to make one fantail biscuit.

In a small bowl, stir together the remaining 2 tablespoons (30 ml) of butter with the mustard.

To assemble a fantail, use a pastry brush to coat the top of one piece of dough with the butter-mustard mixture. Add a slice of Swiss cheese. Top the cheese with a second piece of dough and a piece of the ham. Then top the ham with another layer of dough, coat that layer with the butter-mustard mixture, and then top it with a second slice of cheese. Place the final piece of dough on the cheese. The order should be: dough, butter-mustard mixture, cheese, dough, ham, dough, butter-mustard mixture, cheese, dough.

Place the fantail sideways into the center of a muffin cavity. Repeat the preceding steps with the remaining ingredients for a total of eight large fantails. Loosely cover the muffin pan with a tea towel and set it in a warm, draft-free location to allow the fantails to rise for 40 to 45 minutes, until they have puffed up.

Preheat the oven to 375°F (190°C). While the oven is preheating, prepare the topping. In a small bowl, stir together the poppy seeds and butter. Evenly spoon the mixture over the fantails.

Place the muffin pan on the oven's middle rack and bake the fantails for 20 to 24 minutes, until they are golden brown. Then set the muffin pan on a wire rack for 10 minutes before removing each fantail.

Meanwhile, make the redeye gravy. Add the coffee to the skillet with the reserved ham grease. Cook the mixture over medium-high heat for 30 seconds, stirring to loosen any ham particles from the skillet. Add the butter and brown sugar. Cook the gravy for 2 to 3 minutes, until it has thickened. Transfer the gravy to a bowl or a cup with a spout. Drizzle the warm redeye gravy over the fantails and serve them.

CHEESY DROP BISCUITS

YIELDS

12 biscuits

2½ cups (313 g) all-purpose flour

2 tsp (8 g) sugar

1 tbsp (15 g) baking powder

¼ tsp baking soda

½ tsp sea salt

1 tsp Old Bay Seasoning

½ tsp paprika

½ tsp garlic powder

½ cup (114 g) unsalted butter, cold and cut into cubes, plus more, melted, for serving

1¼ cups (105 g) grated extra sharp Cheddar cheese

1 cup (240 ml) full-fat buttermilk, well shaken

½ cup (120 ml) light beer

Let's talk about another love of mine, seafood. I've spent many days in the summer flounder-gigging, crabbing, and surf fishing on the North Carolina coast. The Outer Banks, Oak Island, and Wrightsville beaches have given me so many fond memories. Every salty-air trip includes a low-country boil with shrimp, sausage, corn, and crab legs. I like to accompany this finger feast with no-fuss cheesy drop biscuits. This biscuit dough is a quick-mix, drop-on-the-pan-and-bake recipe that yields buttery bread in about twenty minutes. Flavored with a little paprika, Old Bay® Seasoning, and beer, these biscuits make for a great evening of fresh seafood on the beach.

Preheat the oven to 425°F (220°C). Line a rimmed large baking sheet with parchment paper.

Whisk together the flour, sugar, baking powder, baking soda, salt, Old Bay Seasoning, paprika, and garlic powder in a large bowl. Add the butter and work it into the flour mixture with a pastry cutter or your fingertips until the flour mixture resembles coarse cornmeal. Fold in the Cheddar cheese and ensure that it is evenly distributed throughout the mixture.

Pour in the buttermilk and beer and stir the batter with a wooden spoon until the ingredients are just combined. Don't overmix the batter; a few streaks of flour are fine.

Use a ¼-cup (60-g) measuring scoop to measure the batter and "drop" the batter onto the prepared baking sheet, spacing each biscuit 2 inches (5 cm) apart. You can gently shape each biscuit into a mound, but they don't have to look perfect. Bake the biscuits on the oven's middle rack for 15 to 17 minutes, until they are light golden brown on top. Serve the biscuits warm with a little melted butter for dipping.

COZY BEER BREAD

1 (9 x 5" [23 x 13–cm]) loaf

3 cups (375 g) self-rising flour

½ tsp sea salt

¼ cup (50 g) sugar

¼ tsp garlic powder

1 tsp minced fresh dill

¼ cup (14 g) jarred oil-packed sun-dried tomatoes, cut into small pieces

½ cup (42 g) grated extra sharp Cheddar cheese

1½ cups (360 ml) amber beer

4 tbsp (56 g) unsalted butter, melted

Beer bread is a recurrent recipe in my kitchen for a quick, savory addition to meals. Beer bread and I first became acquainted when I tried a dough mix that I purchased at a small country store in the mountains. After devouring almost half the loaf that afternoon, I decided it was imperative that I learn how to make it from scratch. I came up with this simple recipe that tastes amazing dipped in soup and chili or slathered with butter.

Preheat the oven to 350°F (180°C). Prepare a 9 x 5–inch (23 x 13–cm) loaf pan with a light coating of nonstick baking spray. Line the bottom and long sides of the loaf pan with overhanging parchment paper for easy removal of the baked loaf.

In a large bowl, whisk together the flour, salt, sugar, garlic powder, and dill. Stir in the sun-dried tomatoes and Cheddar cheese until they are evenly dispersed throughout the mixture. Slowly pour in the beer and stir the mixture just enough to create a thick batter.

Transfer the batter to the prepared loaf pan. Pour the butter on top of the batter and place the loaf pan on the oven's middle rack. Bake the bread for 45 to 50 minutes, until a toothpick inserted into the center comes out with just a few crumbs.

Place the loaf pan on a wire rack to completely cool. Remove the loaf by pulling up on the overhanging parchment paper. Place the loaf on a cutting board and slice it. Serve the bread warm.

BLUEBERRY BANANA BREAD

1 (9 x 5" [23 x 13–cm]) loaf

½ cup (114 g) unsalted butter

1 tbsp (3 g) dried culinary lavender petals (see Notes)

2¼ cups (281 g) plus 1 tbsp (8 g) all-purpose flour, divided

1 tsp baking soda

½ tsp ground ginger

½ tsp sea salt

¼ cup (50 g) granulated sugar

1 tbsp (6 g) fresh lemon zest

¾ packed cup (165 g) light brown sugar

2 cups (454 g) mashed ripe banana

2 large eggs

½ cup (120 ml) whole milk, at room temperature

2 tsp (10 ml) pure vanilla extract

¾ cup (143 g) fresh blueberries, cut in half, plus more as needed

NOTES

Culinary lavender can be purchased from most specialty grocery stores and spice shops.

If you're sensitive to lavender, start with just 1 teaspoon.

Everyone needs a good banana bread recipe in their back pocket. This one is easy to whip up and works great as a "Howdy, neighbor" gift, plus it gives purpose to the forgotten fruit on your counter. This bread combines the familiarity of blueberry muffins and banana bread with the elegance of lavender. Slather whipped honey or some Orange Butter (page 111) on a warm slice.

Preheat the oven to 350°F (180°C). Line a 9 x 5–inch (23 x 13–cm) loaf pan with parchment paper, ensuring that the parchment paper hangs over the long sides of the pan.

In a medium skillet over medium heat, combine the butter and lavender. Cook the mixture for 2 to 3 minutes, until the lavender is fragrant and the butter has slightly browned. Remove the skillet from the heat and strain the butter through a mesh sieve to remove the lavender. Set the butter aside to cool.

In a medium bowl, whisk together 2¼ cups (281 g) of the flour, the baking soda, ginger, and salt. Set the flour mixture aside.

In a large bowl, combine the granulated sugar with the lemon zest and let the mixture sit for 2 minutes. Add the light brown sugar and lavender butter, then whisk the ingredients together until they are combined. Next, whisk in the banana, the eggs—one at a time—the whole milk, and the vanilla.

Using a rubber spatula, fold in the flour mixture ½ cup (63 g) at a time, being careful not to overwork the batter.

Place the blueberries in a small bowl and toss them with the remaining 1 tablespoon (8 g) of flour. This helps prevent the berries from sinking to the bottom of your loaf. Fold the blueberries into the batter, ensuring that they are evenly distributed.

Transfer the batter to the prepared loaf pan, then sprinkle the top of the batter with additional blueberries. Place the pan in the center of the oven's middle rack. Bake the bread for 65 to 70 minutes, until a toothpick inserted into the center comes out mostly clean with a few moist crumbs. Place the loaf pan on a wire rack for 10 minutes before lifting the loaf from the pan by pulling upward on the overhanging parchment paper. Slice the loaf and serve it warm.

CHOCOLATE-ROSEMARY BREAD

YIELDS

1 (9 x 5" [23 x 13–cm]) loaf

BREAD

2 cups (250 g) all-purpose flour

½ cup (43 g) Dutch-process dark cocoa powder, sifted

½ tsp baking powder

1 tsp baking soda

½ tsp sea salt

¼ tsp ground cardamom

¼ tsp ground cinnamon

1 tbsp (6 g) minced fresh rosemary

½ cup (114 g) unsalted butter

½ cup (100 g) granulated sugar

½ cup (110 g) dark brown sugar

½ cup (85 g) finely chopped dark chocolate

2 tsp (10 ml) pure vanilla extract

2 large eggs, at room temperature and lightly beaten

1 cup (240 g) unsweetened applesauce, at room temperature

½ cup (120 ml) plain yogurt, at room temperature

½ cup (85 g) roughly chopped dark chocolate

CHOCOLATE FROSTING

6 tbsp (84 g) unsalted butter

¼ cup (60 ml) whole milk

¼ cup (21 g) unsweetened cocoa powder

2 cups (240 g) confectioners' sugar

The first herb I ever grew in my little garden was rosemary. I immediately became obsessed and started adding it to almost every recipe. It's still my most-loved herb, and if you've read enough of my recipes, you'll know that I use it often.

My other addiction is dark chocolate—that bitterness makes my taste buds tingle. I always keep a bar in the fridge for craving emergencies. If you're prone to snacking on chocolate while gardening, you're going to love the combo in this easy quick bread. Top it with my chocolate frosting for a little extra sweetness.

Preheat the oven to 350°F (180°C). Prepare a 9 x 5–inch (23 x 13–cm) loaf pan with a light coating of nonstick baking spray. Line the bottom and long sides of the pan with overhanging parchment paper.

To make the bread, whisk together the flour, dark cocoa powder, baking powder, baking soda, salt, cardamom, cinnamon, and rosemary in a medium bowl. Set the flour mixture aside.

Cut the butter into ½-inch (1.3-cm) chunks and place the chunks in a medium skillet over medium heat. Cook the butter for about 5 to 6 minutes or until it's golden brown and fragrant, stirring to make sure it cooks evenly. Remove the butter from the heat and let it cool for 10 minutes. The butter should be warm but not scalding hot.

In a large bowl, stir together the granulated sugar and brown sugar. Add the warm browned butter and whisk the ingredients to form a paste. Stir in the finely chopped dark chocolate. Let some of the chocolate pieces soften and slightly melt. One ingredient at a time, pour in the vanilla, eggs, applesauce, and yogurt, whisking just enough to mix in each ingredient.

Finally, spoon the flour mixture into the chocolate mixture in three additions, whisking slowly between each addition to incorporate the ingredients.

Transfer the batter to the prepared loaf pan. Sprinkle the roughly chopped dark chocolate on top of the batter. Bake the bread in the center of the oven's middle rack for 60 to 65 minutes, until it is domed on the top and a toothpick inserted into the center comes out with just a few crumbs.

(CONTINUED)

CHOCOLATE-ROSEMARY BREAD (CONTINUED)

Place the loaf pan on a wire rack to completely cool. Remove the loaf by pulling up on the overhanging parchment paper. Place the loaf on a serving tray.

To make the chocolate frosting, place the butter in a medium skillet over medium heat. Cook the butter for 5 to 6 minutes, until it is golden brown and fragrant. Immediately reduce the heat to low. Add the milk, continually stirring the mixture with a whisk as you sprinkle in the cocoa powder. Continue to stir the mixture for 1 to 2 minutes, or until it has thickened. Remove the sauce from the heat and transfer it to a large bowl. Add ½ cup (60 g) of confectioners' sugar at a time, beating the mixture with a handheld mixer at medium-high speed, until a thick, spreadable frosting forms. If you like a thinner frosting, use only 1 cup (120 g) of the confectioners' sugar. For a thicker frosting, use the full 2 cups (240 g) of confectioners' sugar.

Spread the chocolate frosting on the cooled loaf of bread. Slice and serve the bread.

CHRISTMAS WREATH BREAD

YIELDS

10 slices

DOUGH

1¼ cup (300 ml) whole milk, warmed to 105 to 110°F (40 to 45°C)

2¼ tsp (7 g) active dry yeast

3 tbsp (45 ml) sourwood honey

6 tbsp (84 g) unsalted butter, melted and slightly cooled

1 large egg

1 egg yolk

1 tbsp (6 g) fresh orange zest

4 cups (500 g) all-purpose flour, sifted, plus more as needed

1 tsp kosher salt

Confectioners' sugar, as needed

FILLING

¼ cup (56 g) unsalted butter, melted and cooled

3 tbsp (42 g) light brown sugar

2 tsp (4 g) ground cinnamon

½ tsp ground nutmeg

½ cup (64 g) dried cranberries, roughly chopped

½ cup (57 g) walnuts, roughly chopped

½ cup (57 g) pecans, roughly chopped

The tradition of opening Christmas stockings filled with ornaments and candy is one very dear to my heart. I cherish the excitement of peering into the long, red sock with white trim for a holiday surprise. The foot of the stocking would be fat from a navel orange, and the knitted toe packed with walnuts and pecans.

When I bake this bread, the flavors of citrus, nuts, and cranberries taste just like Christmas morning. Let the aroma fill your house, and share a slice with those you love.

To make the dough, stir together the warm milk, yeast, and honey in the bowl of a stand mixer fitted with the paddle attachment. Let the mixture sit for 8 to 10 minutes, until it is frothy. Add the butter, egg, egg yolk, and orange zest, then mix the ingredients at medium speed for 30 seconds, until they are smooth.

In a medium bowl, whisk together the flour and salt. Lightly grease a large bowl with oil and set it aside.

Fit the stand mixer with the dough hook attachment. With the mixer running at medium-low speed, spoon the flour mixture into the yeast mixture. Once all the flour has been added, increase the mixer's speed to medium-high and work the dough for 5 to 8 minutes. The dough should be smooth but tacky and pull away from the sides of the bowl. Transfer the dough to the prepared bowl, cover the bowl with plastic wrap, and place it in a warm, draft-free location to allow the dough to rise for about 2 hours, until it has doubled in size.

Prepare the filling by stirring together the butter, light brown sugar, cinnamon, and nutmeg in a small bowl. Set the bowl aside.

Lightly dust a work surface with flour. Then lightly coat the top of your hand with flour. Gently press down into the center of the dough with your floured fist to release any excess air. Transfer the dough to the prepared work surface. Roll out the dough to a 20 x 12–inch (51 x 30–cm) rectangle.

Carefully spread the filling paste in a thin layer over the dough, leaving a 1-inch (2.5-cm) border around the edges. Sprinkle the cranberries, walnuts, and pecans over the filling paste. Roll the dough tightly into a long cylinder, pinching the seam closed with your fingers. Carefully slide the cylinder onto a large piece of parchment paper.

(CONTINUED)

CHRISTMAS WREATH BREAD (CONTINUED)

Using a sharp knife, cut the dough lengthwise down the middle. Rotate the two pieces upward to expose the filling. Starting at the top, alternate over and under, braiding the two pieces of dough. If some of the filling spills out, simply push it back in. Connect the ends into a ring shape, overlapping to keep the braided shape that resembles a large wreath.

Slide the parchment paper and dough wreath onto a large baking sheet. Cover the wreath with a light tea towel and let it rest for 45 minutes in a warm location to puff up.

Meanwhile, preheat the oven to 350°F (180°C).

Bake the wreath on the oven's center rack for 25 to 30 minutes, until it is golden brown and beginning to get crispy on top. Place the baking sheet on a wire rack to cool for 10 minutes before slicing the bread. Dust the bread lightly with the confectioners' sugar for a snow effect just prior to serving it.

NOTE

A fun way to display your wreath bread before serving is to let it cool completely, then tie a ribbon at the seam. If you're making it as a holiday gift, place the wreath inside a clear, food-safe wrapping bag and tie it closed with another ribbon.

Morning Sweets and Snacks

I look forward to a big weekend breakfast as much as I do sleeping in until midday. So I guess that means I love brunch, right? Slow mornings with no agenda other than cooking and lounging about, enjoying the fruits of your kitchen labor, is true bliss. My favorite breakfasts include a little bit of everything: salty pork, eggs, sweet toppings, and buttermilk-infused baked goods.

My breakfast menu always changes but never strays too far from taste-tested favorites. Maple-applewood bacon, country ham, and spicy pork sausage are at the top of the protein list. Next, there must be cheese—rich yellow hoop cheese or goat cheese from the farmers' market. Fresh eggs make an appearance, whether they are sunny-side up, scrambled, or—even better—in a quiche. Then there is the local sourwood honey, blackberry preserves, and fluffy warm biscuits. Are you hungry yet?

I love a flaky biscuit sandwich layered with country ham, Cheddar cheese, extra jelly, and a serving of eggs, maybe with a side of grits doused in redeye gravy. Not to mention molasses and butter on warm muffins still steaming as you tear them open. Maybe breakfast truly is the best meal of the day. Just don't mention that to the desserts.

What I love the most about the recipes in this chapter are the memories they evoke: My dad teaching me how to wait for the center bubbles to appear in pancakes before flipping them over, then gently placing them in his green pancake warmer with little metal feet until it was time to eat. Spinning the lazy Susan on my grandmother's breakfast table to find the jar of fresh peach preserves. My mom wrapping blueberry muffins in a linen-lined woven basket like fragile ornaments. And waking up to the smell of hot cinnamon rolls that flooded the house on a holiday morning as I rushed to the kitchen in my pajamas.

The following breakfast recipes are reflections of my favorite flavors of simple morning indulgences. They follow no-fuss steps that will make a weekend breakfast deliciously enjoyable while you relax.

TIPS FOR SUCCESS

- Make sure your eggs, milk, and buttermilk are at room temperature unless the recipe specifically calls for something hot or cold.

- When baking jumbo muffins, fill every other muffin cavity to allow the hot air to move around the muffins—this will result in bigger tops on your muffins. Store the muffins in an airtight container lined with a paper towel. The paper towel will help keep the muffins from getting soggy.

- Morning Honey Rolls (page 151) and Pecan Sticky Whirls (page 153) can be made the night before and stored in the fridge until you're ready to bake them the next morning.

FLUFFY BREAKFAST BISCUITS

YIELDS

6 large biscuits

3 cups (375 g) all-purpose flour, plus more as needed

2 tbsp (30 g) baking powder

½ tsp baking soda

½ tsp sea salt

1 cup (227 g) unsalted butter, cold and cut into ½" (1.3-cm) cubes, plus more, melted, as needed

¾ cup (180 ml) plain Greek yogurt

¼ cup (60 ml) plus 2 tbsp (30 ml) heavy cream, plus more as needed

NOTE

Store the biscuits at room temperature in an airtight container for 2 days, if you don't devour them all at once.

When you think of a southern breakfast, do you think of biscuits? I mean, making homemade biscuits is a requirement to be a southern baker. Classic biscuits are usually made with buttermilk, but this recipe uses a Greek yogurt twist that also results in large, fluffy layers with a lovely tang. Cutting the biscuits in a square shape makes prep easier without wasting any dough. They're perfect for a breakfast sandwich with a slice of country ham, some Cheddar cheese, and an over-easy egg. Or just drench them in your favorite honey, like I do.

Get your biscuit-baking groove on by preheating the oven to 450°F (230°C). Line a large baking sheet with parchment paper or a silicone baking mat.

In a large bowl, whisk together the flour, baking powder, baking soda, and salt. Add the butter and, using a pastry cutter or your fingertips, work the butter into the flour mixture until its texture resembles cornmeal, leaving pea-sized bits of butter.

In a small bowl, whisk together the Greek yogurt and heavy cream. Pour the yogurt-cream mixture into the flour mixture. Using a wooden spoon or rubber spatula, gently combine the ingredients. Shape the dough into a ball with your hands. If the dough is too dry and not quite coming together, add 1 tablespoon (15 ml) of heavy cream, but be careful not to make the dough soggy.

Lightly dust a work surface with flour. Transfer the dough to the prepared work surface. Using flat hands, pat the dough out until it is a rectangle about ½ inch (1.3 cm) thick. Cut the dough into fourths. Stack the four pieces on top of one another.

With a rolling pin, gently roll the stack of dough into another rectangle, this time 1 inch (2.5 cm) in thickness. Cut the rectangle in half lengthwise with a sharp knife, and then cut it into thirds. This should give you six large square biscuits.

Place the six biscuits on the prepared baking sheet, spacing them 2 inches (5 cm) apart. Gently brush the tops of the biscuits with additional heavy cream. Bake the biscuits for 12 to 15 minutes, until they are fluffy and golden brown on the edges.

Remove the baking sheet from the oven and place it on a wire rack. Brush the biscuits with the melted butter and serve them warm.

CHORIZO-JALAPEÑO SCONES

1 cup (125 g) all-purpose flour

1 cup (125 g) bread flour

½ tsp kosher salt

1 tbsp (15 g) baking powder

4 tbsp (56 g) unsalted butter, cold and cut into small cubes

½ cup (120 ml) plus 3 tbsp (45 ml) heavy cream, plus more as needed

1 large egg, lightly beaten

½ cup (42 g) grated smoked Gouda cheese or extra sharp Cheddar cheese, plus more as needed

2 fresh jalapeños, stems and seeds removed, finely chopped (see Note)

½ cup (98 g) ground chorizo, cooked and drained

You're going to love this savory blend of spicy jalapeño, salty chorizo, and rich smoked Gouda! Savory scones are one of my favorite bakery items. While living in Nashville, I became addicted to jalapeño scones from the local bakery in my east-side neighborhood. This area, jokingly referred to as East Nasty, is the trendiest foodie area around. My beloved morning eatery used large, chunky bits of peppers, an approach I've replicated in this recipe along with extra cheese to balance the chorizo. A spicy little breakfast pastry is always a good idea, especially if you top it with an over-easy egg.

Preheat the oven to 425°F (220°C). Line a rimmed large baking sheet with parchment paper or a silicone mat.

In a large bowl, whisk together the all-purpose flour, bread flour, salt, and baking powder. Add the butter cubes and work them into the flour with a pastry cutter or your fingers until the mixture resembles cornmeal.

In a small bowl, stir together the heavy cream and egg. Pour this mixture into the flour mixture. Add the Gouda cheese and mix the ingredients together with a wooden spoon until they are just combined. Gently fold in the jalapeños and chorizo with your hands to evenly distribute them into the batter. Knead the batter a couple of times just to form a dough, being careful not to overwork the dough.

Transfer the dough to the prepared baking sheet. With your hands, pat the dough into a 10- to 12-inch (25- to 30-cm) circle. With a sharp knife or pastry scraper, cut the dough across its diameter to make four pieces of dough. Cut each piece of dough in half lengthwise to make a total of 8 triangles. Space the scones about 2 inches (5 cm) apart on the baking sheet.

Using a pastry brush, add a light coating of additional heavy cream to the tops of the scones. Sprinkle the scones with extra cheese. Place the baking sheet in the center of the oven's middle rack and bake them for 18 to 20 minutes, or until they are light golden brown. Serve the scones warm with a side of eggs.

NOTE

Always wear food-prep gloves when working with spicy peppers to prevent accidentally burning your eyes should you touch them after handling the peppers.

BLUEBERRY BUTTERMILK MALT PANCAKES

YIELDS

12 pancakes

2½ cups (313 g) all-purpose flour

¼ cup (50 g) sugar

2 tsp (10 g) baking powder

1 tsp baking soda

½ tsp kosher salt

2 tbsp (10 g) malted milk powder

½ tsp ground cinnamon

3 large eggs, at room temperature and lightly beaten

½ tsp pure vanilla extract

2½ cups (600 ml) full-fat buttermilk, at room temperature

⅓ cup (76 g) unsalted butter, melted and cooled, plus more, cold, as needed

1 cup (190 g) fresh blueberries

Maple syrup, for serving

Blueberry pancakes was the very first recipe I learned to make with the guidance of my breakfast-loving dad. Yep, he is a pancake connoisseur and prepares them for everyone's birthday and slow weekend mornings with a side of maple sausage. He taught me that a bubble in the center of the pancake indicates that it's time to flip the pancake over. Thanks, Dad. The key ingredients to the success of these pancakes are fresh blueberries, malted milk powder, and, of course, buttermilk.

In a medium bowl, whisk together the flour, sugar, baking powder, baking soda, salt, malted milk powder, and cinnamon.

In a large bowl, whisk together the eggs and vanilla. Pour in the buttermilk and butter, stirring until the ingredients are combined. Add half of the flour mixture at a time to the buttermilk mixture and whisk the two mixtures until they are just combined. Don't overmix your batter; a few lumps and streaks of flour are fine. Let the batter rest for about 20 minutes.

Heat a large nonstick or cast-iron skillet over low heat for about 5 minutes. Add 1 tablespoon (15 g) of the cold butter to the skillet. As the butter melts, tilt the skillet to evenly coat the bottom. Increase the heat to medium-low and, using a measuring cup, pour ⅓ cup (80 ml) of the pancake batter into the skillet. Sprinkle the batter with 5 or 6 blueberries, being careful to keep them away from the edges of the batter so they don't fall out when you flip the pancake.

Watch the center of the pancake, looking for small bubbles to appear—this will take 2 to 3 minutes. Carefully flip your pancake over and cook it for about 1 minute, until the other side is light brown. Remove the pancake from the skillet and place it in a pancake warmer or directly on a serving dish.

Repeat the preceding steps with the remaining batter and blueberries, using more butter for the skillet as needed.

Serve two or three pancakes in a stack with a generous amount of warm maple syrup.

BACON, APPLE, AND CHEDDAR WAFFLES

YIELDS

12 waffles

2¼ cups (281 g) all-purpose flour

1 tbsp (15 g) baking powder

1 tbsp (13 g) sugar

½ tsp kosher salt

1¾ cups (420 ml) full-fat buttermilk, at room temperature

½ cup (114 g) unsalted butter, melted and cooled

2 large eggs, at room temperature and lightly beaten

1½ cups (126 g) grated extra sharp Cheddar cheese

1 cup (118 g) shredded Granny Smith apples

36 strips maplewood bacon

Maple syrup, for serving

Cheddar cheese on top of a Granny Smith apple pie is a common southern combo. That little bit of cinnamon with the hot pastry and cheese really is delicious. It wasn't until I was dipping a bacon, apple, and cheese sandwich in maple syrup that I decided waffles would work too. I've completely converted to sweet and savory waffles, and I've found that using whole strips of bacon provides a bit of all three flavors in every bite!

In a medium bowl, whisk together the flour, baking powder, sugar, and salt.

In a large bowl, whisk together the buttermilk, butter, and eggs. Add half of the flour mixture at a time to the buttermilk mixture and whisk the two mixtures until they are just combined. Don't overmix your batter; a few lumps and streaks of flour are fine. Fold in the Cheddar cheese and apples. Let the batter rest for about 20 minutes.

Lightly spray a Belgian waffle iron with nonstick cooking spray. Place 3 strips of the bacon directly on the waffle iron. Close the waffle iron and cook the bacon for 4 minutes. Open the waffle iron and pour about ¾ cup (180 ml) of the waffle batter over the strips of bacon. Close the waffle iron, flip it, and cook the waffle according to the manufacturer's directions. My waffles cook for 7 to 8 minutes.

Remove the waffle from the waffle iron and place it in a pancake warmer or directly on a serving tray. Repeat the preceding steps with the remaining bacon and waffle batter, greasing the waffle iron with more nonstick cooking spray as needed.

Serve the waffles with warm maple syrup.

LEMON-CHERRY
GOOD MORNING MUFFINS

YIELDS

6 jumbo muffins

MUFFINS

1 cup (140 g) fresh bing cherries, pitted and roughly chopped (see Note)

1¼ cups (156 g) plus 2 tsp (6 g) all-purpose flour, divided

1 cup (125 g) cake flour

1 tbsp (15 g) baking powder

¼ tsp baking soda

½ tsp kosher salt

1 cup (200 g) granulated sugar

2 tbsp (12 g) fresh lemon zest

½ tsp ground ginger

2 tbsp (30 ml) fresh lemon juice

½ cup (114 g) unsalted butter, at room temperature

2 large eggs

⅔ cup (160 ml) full-fat buttermilk

TOPPING

¼ cup (35 g) roughly chopped fresh bing cherries

1 tbsp (12 g) sparkling sugar

¼ tsp ground ginger

NOTE

I tested different sizes of chopped cherries, and small pieces the size of a raisin that have been lightly coated in flour are best to prevent all your cherries from sinking to the bottom of the muffins.

When cherries are in season, I find myself snacking on them all day. Red-stained hands are a good indication of fresh juicy fruit in the fridge. I've always made pies with fresh cherries, but I have also found that they are delicious in muffins. The mixture of fresh, sweet bing cherries and lemons in a sugar-topped treat is a delicious way to start your morning.

Begin your muffin breakfast by preheating the oven to 425°F (220°C). Prepare a 6-cavity jumbo muffin pan with a light coating of nonstick baking spray. Alternatively, line the muffin cavities with large paper liners.

To make the muffins, place the cherries in a medium bowl and toss them with 2 teaspoons (6 g) of the all-purpose flour to evenly coat them. Set the bowl of cherries aside.

In another medium bowl, whisk together the remaining 1¼ cups (156 g) all-purpose flour, the cake flour, baking powder, baking soda, and salt. Set this flour mixture aside.

In a large bowl, whisk together the granulated sugar, lemon zest, ginger, and lemon juice until the ingredients are combined. Add the butter to the sugar mixture and beat the two together with a handheld mixer at medium-high speed for 2 to 3 minutes, until the mixture is fluffy. Add the eggs and beat the ingredients at medium speed for 30 to 60 seconds, until the ingredients are mixed together. With the handheld mixer running at medium-low speed, spoon in half of the flour mixture, alternating it with ⅓ cup (80 ml) of the buttermilk. Repeat this process with the remaining half of the flour mixture and the remaining ⅓ cup (80 ml) buttermilk. Fold in the flour-coated cherries until they are evenly distributed. Divide the batter among the prepared muffin cavities.

To prepare the topping, sprinkle the cherries across the top of each muffin. In a small bowl, stir together the sparkling sugar and ginger. Sprinkle this mixture on the top of each muffin.

Place the muffin pan on the oven's middle rack and bake the muffins for 5 minutes. Reduce the oven's temperature to 350°F (180°C) and bake the muffins for 25 to 28 minutes, until their edges are light golden brown. When you lightly touch the top of a muffin with your finger, it should spring back, and a toothpick inserted into the center should come out clean with just a few crumbs.

Remove the muffin pan from the oven and place it on a wire rack for 15 minutes. Gently remove the muffins by running a knife around the muffins' edges and tilting the pan on its side. Serve the muffins warm.

FARMERS' MARKET MUFFINS

⅓ cup (76 g) unsalted butter

2 cups (250 g) whole-wheat flour

1 tsp baking powder

2 tsp (10 g) baking soda

2 tsp (4 g) ground cinnamon

½ tsp ground ginger

½ tsp kosher salt

¾ packed cup (165 g) brown sugar

3 large eggs, lightly beaten

1 large egg yolk

2 tbsp (30 ml) pure maple syrup

⅓ cup (80 ml) fresh pineapple juice

2 tsp (10 ml) pure vanilla extract

2 cups (236 g) shredded Pink Lady apples

½ cup (64 g) dried sweet cherries, roughly chopped

½ cup (57 g) walnut halves, roughly chopped

My Saturday mornings are spent strolling through farmers' markets, sipping on chai and eating locally baked muffins. Collecting produce and meats while tasting the vendors' samples is the perfect start to the weekend. The Old Salem Cobblestone Farmers Market in North Carolina, nestled among colonial homes, is where I fell in love with morning glory muffins. This recipe is quite similar to traditional morning glory muffins, using whole-wheat flour with brown sugar and apples instead of carrots.

Preheat the oven to 375°F (190°C). Prepare a 12-cavity muffin pan with a light coating of nonstick baking spray, or line each cavity with paper liners.

Place the butter in a medium, light-colored skillet over medium heat. Stir the butter as it melts. It will foam and start to sizzle. Continue to stir the butter for 5 to 7 minutes, until it starts to turn a golden-brown color. The foam will begin to dissipate and solid brown milk dots will form at the bottom of the skillet. The browned butter should have a lovely nutty aroma. Immediately transfer the browned butter to a heatproof medium bowl to prevent it from cooking any further. Let the browned butter cool.

In a medium bowl, whisk together the flour, baking powder, baking soda, cinnamon, ginger, and salt. Set this flour mixture aside.

In a large bowl, whisk together the brown sugar, eggs, egg yolk, browned butter, maple syrup, pineapple juice, and vanilla until the ingredients are smooth. Stir in the apples with a rubber spatula to distribute them throughout the mixture. Stir in half of the flour mixture, slowly stirring with a rubber spatula, until it is just combined with the apple mixture. Repeat this process with the remaining half of the flour mixture. A few streaks of flour are fine. Fold in the cherries and walnuts.

Divide the batter among the muffin cavities. Place the muffin pan on the oven's middle rack. Bake the muffins for 23 to 25 minutes, until their edges are light golden brown. When you lightly touch the top of a muffin with your finger, it should spring back, and a toothpick inserted into the center of a muffin should come out clean with just a few crumbs.

Remove the muffin pan from the oven and place it on a wire rack for 15 minutes. Gently remove the muffins from the pan by tilting the pan on its side. Serve the muffins warm.

CHOCOHOLIC MUFFINS

YIELDS

6 jumbo muffins

2 cups (250 g) all-purpose flour

½ cup (43 g) unsweetened dark cocoa powder

2 tsp (10 g) baking powder

½ tsp sea salt

1 tsp ground cinnamon

¾ cup (150 g) granulated sugar

¼ packed cup (55 g) light brown sugar

½ cup (120 ml) neutral oil

2 large eggs

½ cup (120 ml) whole milk, at room temperature

2 tbsp (30 ml) Greek yogurt, room temperature

¼ cup (60 ml) strong brewed coffee, at room temperature

2 tsp (10 ml) pure vanilla extract

1 cup (170 g) roughly chopped semisweet chocolate, divided

Turbinado sugar, as needed

NOTE

For the best results to the tops of your muffins, use two muffins pans and fill every other muffin cavity. This spaces the muffins apart and allows warm air to move around the tops. Bake one pan of muffins at a time.

I'm not sure how southern chocolate muffins are, though I've spent years enjoying them at horse shows and antique shows. When I trained jumping horses, I would walk through the showgrounds before dawn with a cup of coffee and a double-chocolate muffin. My days were always better when I started them with chocolate. These muffins are big, moist, and full of cocoa for the chocoholic on the go.

Preheat the oven to 400°F (200°C). Prepare a 6-cavity jumbo muffin pan with a light coating of nonstick baking spray, or line each cavity with large paper liners.

In a medium bowl, whisk together the flour, cocoa powder, baking powder, salt, and cinnamon. Set this flour mixture aside.

In the bowl of a stand mixer fitted with the paddle attachment, mix together the granulated sugar, brown sugar, and oil at medium speed until combined. Reduce the mixer's speed to low and add the eggs one at a time. Scrape the sides and bottom of the bowl. Add the milk, Greek yogurt, coffee, and vanilla, mixing at low speed to combine the ingredients. Remove the bowl from the stand mixer.

Fold one-third of the flour mixture into the batter at a time, slowly mixing with a rubber spatula until the ingredients are just combined. Don't stir or overmix the batter. A few streaks of flour are fine. After you have folded in all of the flour mixture, fold in ½ cup (85 g) of the chocolate. Cover the bowl with a tea towel and let the batter rest for 30 minutes.

Divide the batter among the muffin cavities, filling each one three-fourths full. Sprinkle the turbinado sugar and the remaining ½ cup (85 g) of the chocolate on the tops of the muffins.

Place the muffin pan on the oven's middle rack and bake the muffins for 22 to 24 minutes. When you lightly touch the top of a muffin with your finger, it should spring back, and a toothpick inserted into the center of a muffin should come out with just a few crumbs.

Remove the muffin pan from the oven and place it on a wire rack for 10 minutes. Gently remove the muffins from the pan by running a knife around the muffins' edges and tilting the pan on its side. Serve the muffins warm.

PEACH OATMEAL CRUNCH MUFFINS

YIELDS
6 jumbo muffins

MUFFINS

1 cup (80 g) old-fashioned oats

1 cup (240 ml) full-fat buttermilk

¼ cup (60 ml) vegetable oil

2 tsp (4 g) ground cinnamon

½ tsp ground nutmeg

2 tsp (10 ml) pure vanilla extract

1 cup (125 g) all-purpose flour

1 cup (125 g) whole-wheat flour

¾ cup (165 g) light brown sugar

¼ cup (50 g) granulated sugar

1 tbsp (15 g) baking powder

½ tsp baking soda

½ tsp kosher salt

2 large eggs, lightly beaten

⅓ cup (76 g) unsalted butter, melted and cooled

1 cup (154 g) peeled, pitted, and roughly chopped fresh yellow peaches, plus ½ fresh yellow peach, peeled, pitted, and thinly sliced

OATMEAL CRUMBLE

⅓ cup (42 g) whole-wheat flour

½ cup (40 g) old-fashioned oats

¼ cup (55 g) light brown sugar

1 tsp ground cinnamon

¼ cup (57 g) unsalted butter, melted and cooled

Fresh yellow peaches are my favorite fruit, and in the summer I eat them every day. I love them in pies, cobblers, milkshakes, on pancakes, and, yes, in my muffins. In this recipe, I'm opting for that delicious brown sugar and cinnamon crumble on top of a peach-filled pastry instead of oatmeal for breakfast. Be sure to pick a bunch of fresh peaches and freeze them for a winter batch of these oatmeal crunch muffins.

Preheat the oven to 425°F (220°C). Lightly grease a 6-cavity muffin pan, or line each cavity with a paper liner and spray the paper liners with a light coating of nonstick baking spray.

To make the muffins, stir together the oats, buttermilk, vegetable oil, cinnamon, nutmeg, and vanilla in a large bowl. Let this mixture rest for 20 minutes.

In a medium bowl, whisk together the all-purpose flour, whole-wheat flour, brown sugar, granulated sugar, baking powder, baking soda, and salt. Set the flour mixture aside.

Add the eggs and butter to the oat-buttermilk mixture and stir to combine the ingredients. Spoon in the flour mixture and, using a rubber spatula, gently mix the ingredients only enough to distribute them evenly. A few small streaks of flour are fine. Fold in the chopped peaches.

Divide the batter evenly among the muffin cavities, filling them three-fourths full. Place a peach slice on the top of each muffin.

To make the oatmeal crumble, use a fork to stir together the whole-wheat flour, oats, brown sugar, cinnamon, and butter in a medium bowl. Sprinkle the crumble on top of each muffin.

Bake the muffins for 5 minutes, then lower the oven temperature to 350°F (180°C) and bake for another 20 to 22 minutes until they are golden brown and a toothpick inserted in the center of a muffin comes out with just a few crumbs. Remove the muffin pan from the oven and place it on a wire rack to cool for 5 minutes before tipping the muffins out of the pan. Place the individual muffins on the rack to cool until they are warm, then serve them.

MORNING HONEY ROLLS

YIELDS

6 large rolls

DOUGH

½ cup (120 ml) whole milk, warmed to 105 to 110°F (40 to 45°C)

2¼ tsp (7 g) active dry yeast

⅓ cup (67 g) granulated sugar, divided

1 cup (125 g) bread flour, sifted

1¼ cups (156 g) all-purpose flour, sifted, plus more as needed

1½ tsp (3 g) ground ginger

¼ tsp kosher salt

4 tbsp (56 g) unsalted butter, melted and cooled, plus more as needed

1 large egg

FILLING

¼ cup (85 g) whipped honey

1 tbsp (14 g) butter, melted and slightly warm

2 tsp (4 g) ground cinnamon

¼ tsp ground ginger

COATING

¼ cup (85 g) whipped honey, warm

FROSTING

1 cup (120 g) confectioners' sugar

1 tbsp (15 ml) pure vanilla extract

5 to 6 tbsp (75 to 90 ml) heavy cream, plus more if needed

"Good morning, honey—have a warm, gooey cinnamon roll!" Aren't those just the best words to wake up to? I first tried whipped honey at a local farm store and was immediately hooked. Whipped honey is honey that has been spun into a smooth, creamy texture. Spreading it on my toast and rolls morphed into adding it to my sweet roll filling. A small batch of honey-ginger pastry topped with vanilla frosting makes any morning that much sweeter.

Make the dough by stirring together the milk, yeast, and 1 tablespoon (13 g) of the granulated sugar in the bowl of a stand mixer fitted with the dough hook attachment. Let this mixture rest for 8 to 10 minutes, until it is frothy.

Meanwhile, in a medium bowl, whisk together the bread flour, all-purpose flour, ginger, and salt. Set the flour mixture aside.

In a small bowl, stir together the butter and remaining granulated sugar until the ingredients are smooth. Pour the butter-sugar mixture into the yeast mixture and mix them together at medium-low speed. Add the egg and mix the ingredients again. Gently scrape the bottom of the bowl with a rubber spatula to make sure all the ingredients are combined.

With the mixer running at medium speed, slowly spoon in the flour mixture. Once all of the flour mixture has been added, increase the mixer's speed to medium-high and work the dough for 5 to 6 minutes. The dough should be slightly tacky, yet smooth, and pull away from the edges of the bowl. If the dough is very sticky, simply add 1 tablespoon (8 g) of additional all-purpose flour to the bowl. Alternatively, you can remove the dough from the bowl and knead it by hand on a floured work surface for 8 to 10 minutes.

Pull off a small piece of the dough and spread it thinly with your fingertips. If you can see light through the dough without it breaking, then there is enough gluten formed and the dough is ready. This is called the windowpane test.

Lightly coat a large bowl with butter. Transfer the dough to the prepared bowl. Cover the bowl with plastic wrap and place it in a warm, draft-free location to allow the dough to rise for 1 to 2 hours, until it has doubled in size.

(CONTINUED)

MORNING HONEY ROLLS (CONTINUED)

Once the dough has doubled in size, remove the plastic wrap from the bowl. Generously dust a work surface with flour. Then lightly dust the top of your hand with flour. With your lightly floured fist, slowly press down into the dough to release any excess air. Transfer the dough to the prepared work surface and lightly dust a rolling pin with flour. Roll the dough into an approximately 10 x 6–inch (25 x 15–cm) rectangle that is about ½ inch (1.3 cm) thick.

Now, make the filling. In a small bowl, stir together the whipped honey, butter, cinnamon, and ginger until a soft, spreadable, slightly thick paste forms. Using a pastry brush or small rubber spatula, gently coat the surface of the dough with the filling, leaving a ¾-inch (2-cm) border of bare dough around the edges. Starting from the long side of the dough, roll it inward to create a tight log. Seal the edges with your fingertips as best you can. You can trim about ½ inch (1.3 cm) off the ends if you like, as they are usually just dough without much filling.

Score the log into six even pieces, then cut the individual pieces using a sharp knife. You can also use a 12-inch (30-cm)-long piece of unflavored dental floss, sliding it under the rolled dough and crossing the ends over the top to cut through the dough and filling.

Line a 9 x 9–inch (23 x 23–cm) baking pan or 9-inch (23-cm) cast-iron skillet with parchment paper. Arrange the rolls swirl side up, exposing the filling, in the prepared baking pan. Allow a little space between each roll, so that they can rise. Cover the rolls with a thin towel and let them rest in a warm location for 30 to 45 minutes, until they have puffed up. You can also place the pan of rolls in a cold oven with the light on. If you choose to make the rolls the day before you want to bake them, cover the baking pan with plastic wrap and refrigerate the rolls for 8 to 12 hours. Allow the cold rolls to warm to room temperature for about 45 minutes before baking them.

Preheat the oven to 350°F (180°C). Gently coat the rolls with the warm whipped honey. Place the pan in the center of the oven's middle rack. Bake the rolls for 25 to 28 minutes, or until they are just starting to brown on top. You can pull them out just a bit underdone for a gooey center. Place the baking pan on a wire rack for 5 minutes while you make the frosting.

To make the frosting, combine the confectioners' sugar, vanilla, and heavy cream in a medium bowl. Stir the ingredients together with a fork. The frosting should be a thick yet spreadable consistency. Add 1 tablespoon (15 ml) of additional heavy cream to make the frosting thinner. Spread the frosting on the warm honey rolls and serve them.

PECAN STICKY WHIRLS

YIELDS

10 to 12 whirls

DOUGH

2¼ tsp (7 g) active dry yeast

1 cup (240 ml) whole milk, warmed to 105 to 110°F (40 to 45°C)

⅓ cup (67 g) granulated sugar, divided

3 cups (375 g) all-purpose flour, sifted, plus more as needed

1 cup (125 g) pastry flour, sifted

1 tsp kosher salt

½ cup (114 g) unsalted butter, softened, plus more as needed

2 large eggs, lightly beaten

FILLING

1 packed cup (220 g) dark brown sugar

2 tbsp (12 g) ground cinnamon

¼ cup (57 g) unsalted butter, melted and slightly warm

½ cup (57 g) pecans, finely chopped

TOPPING

¼ cup (57 g) unsalted butter, plus more as needed

¾ packed cup (165 g) dark brown sugar

3 tbsp (45 ml) pure maple syrup

1½ cups (170 g) pecans, roughly chopped

2 tbsp (30 ml) warm honey

My family loves to tell the story of the great grocery store search for "wan whirls." Apparently I was too young to say "pecan twirls," and no one knew what I was talking about. Anytime a pecan is mentioned, my parents tell this story. Gooey, sticky buns covered in melted brown sugar and pecans have now taken their place. These indulgent breakfast rolls are best enjoyed fresh from the oven.

To make the dough, stir together the yeast, milk, and 1 tablespoon (13 g) of the granulated sugar in the bowl of a stand mixer fitted with the paddle attachment. Let the mixture rest for 8 to 10 minutes, until it is frothy.

Meanwhile, in a medium bowl, whisk together the all-purpose flour, pastry flour, and salt. Set the flour mixture aside.

Add the remaining granulated sugar, butter, and eggs to the yeast mixture. Mix the ingredients at medium-low speed until they are combined. Gently scrape the bottom of the bowl with a rubber spatula to make sure all the ingredients are combined.

Fit the stand mixer with the dough hook attachment and turn the mixer to medium speed. Slowly spoon in the flour mixture. Once all of the flour has been added, increase the mixer's speed to medium-high and work the dough for 5 to 6 minutes. The dough should be slightly tacky yet smooth and pull away from the edges of the bowl. If the dough is very sticky, simply add 1 tablespoon (8 g) of additional all-purpose flour to the bowl. Alternatively, you can knead the dough by hand on a floured work surface for 8 to 10 minutes.

Pull off a small piece of the dough and spread it thinly with your fingertips. If you can see light through the dough without it breaking, then there is enough gluten formed and the dough is ready. This is called the windowpane test.

Lightly grease a large bowl with butter. Transfer the dough to the prepared bowl. Cover the bowl with plastic wrap and place it in a warm, draft-free location for 1 to 2 hours, until the dough has doubled in size.

(CONTINUED)

PECAN STICKY WHIRLS (CONTINUED)

Once the dough has doubled in size, remove the plastic wrap. Generously dust a work surface with flour. Then lightly coat the top of your hand with flour. With your lightly floured fist, slowly press down into the dough to release any excess air. Transfer the dough to the prepared work surface. Lightly dust a rolling pin with flour, then roll the dough into an approximately 16 x 20–inch (41 x 51–cm) rectangle that is about ¼ inch (6 mm) thick.

To make the filling, stir together the brown sugar and cinnamon in a small bowl. Use a pastry brush to gently coat the surface of the dough with the butter, leaving a ¾-inch (2-cm) border of bare dough around the edges. Sprinkle the cinnamon sugar over the butter, then sprinkle the pecans over the cinnamon sugar.

Starting from the long side of the dough, roll it inward to create a tight log. Seal the edges with your fingertips as best you can. You can trim about ½ inch (1.3 cm) off the ends of the dough log if you like, as they are usually just dough without much filling.

Score the log into 12 even pieces, then use a sharp knife to cut the individual rolls. You can also use a 12-inch (30-cm)-long piece of unflavored dental floss, sliding it under the rolled dough and crossing the ends over the top to cut through the dough and filling.

Prepare the topping by placing the butter, brown sugar, and maple syrup in a medium saucepan over low heat. Cook the mixture for 2 to 3 minutes, stirring it occasionally, until the butter and brown sugar are melted.

Lightly coat a 9 x 13–inch (23 x 33–cm) baking pan with butter. Pour the topping mixture into the prepared baking pan. Sprinkle the topping mixture with the pecans. Arrange the cut rolls swirl side up, exposing the filling to the pecans.

Cover the baking pan with a thin towel and allow the rolls to rest in a warm location for 30 to 45 minutes, until they have puffed up. You can also place them in a cold oven with the light on. If you choose to make the rolls the day before you want to bake them, cover the baking pan with plastic wrap and refrigerate the rolls for 8 to 12 hours. Allow them to warm at room temperature for about 45 minutes before baking them.

Preheat the oven to 375°F (190°C). Gently brush the honey over the rolls. Place the baking pan in the center of the oven's middle rack. Bake the rolls for 30 to 35 minutes, or until they are just starting to brown on top. You can pull them out just a bit underdone for a gooey center.

Remove the baking pan from the oven and immediately invert it on a large serving dish. I prefer to use a rimmed large baking sheet: Place the baking sheet on top of the baking pan and then flip the baking pan over, holding on to the baking sheet as you do so. Lift the baking pan away from the rolls—the hot pecan topping will slide over the top and the sides of the rolls. Let the rolls cool for about 5 minutes before serving them.

SKILLET GRANOLA

YIELDS

About 3 cups (720 g)

¼ cup (60 ml) amber pure maple syrup

1 tsp pure vanilla extract

¼ tsp pure almond extract

½ tsp ground cinnamon

¼ tsp sea salt

3 tbsp (45 ml) sunflower seed oil

¼ cup (28 g) pecan halves, roughly chopped

¼ cup (28 g) black walnut halves, roughly chopped

¼ cup (48 g) small pumpkin seeds

1½ cups (120 g) old-fashioned oats

½ cup (64 g) dried sweet cherries

The easiest homemade snack to put on top of yogurt, pancakes, desserts, or fruit has to be skillet granola. When I was growing up in North Carolina, we always had an abundance of pecans and black walnuts, which meant we had to make something other than pies. Mixed-nut granola with dried fruit is easy to make and disappears just as quickly as a pie. Use a cast-iron skillet on the stove or over a campfire. I always keep a glass jar full of granola in my kitchen, and I have a travel bag stuffed with it for snacking during all my outdoor activities.

Line a large baking sheet with a silicone baking mat or parchment paper. Set the baking sheet aside.

In a small bowl, whisk together the maple syrup, vanilla, almond extract, cinnamon, and salt. Set the maple mixture aside.

Heat the oil in a medium cast-iron skillet over medium heat. Add the pecans, walnuts, and pumpkin seeds, then use a heatproof rubber spatula to fold them into the oil, coating them evenly. Cook the mixture for 3 to 4 minutes, stirring it slowly, until the nuts and seeds are fragrant and beginning to darken in color. If you find they are cooking too quickly, reduce the heat to medium-low.

Add the oats to the skillet. Cook the mixture, continuing to stir it, for about 6 minutes, until the oats are golden in color. Pour in the maple mixture and add the cherries. Stir the entire mixture slowly for about 3 minutes, until it's a bit darker and well mixed.

Transfer the granola to the prepared baking sheet and let it cool. Then transfer it to an airtight container for storage. Eat the granola plain, sprinkle it on yogurt or ice cream, or use it as a topping on your favorite pie.

SPICY CHEESE STRAWS

YIELDS

2 dozen

2 cups (250 g) all-purpose flour, plus more as needed

1 tsp sea salt

¾ tsp red pepper flakes

¾ tsp paprika

¼ tsp cayenne pepper

¼ tsp onion powder

1 cup (227 g) unsalted butter, cut into ½" (1.3-cm) cubes, at room temperature

2 cups (168 g) grated extra sharp Cheddar cheese, at room temperature

2 tbsp (30 ml) whole milk

Cheese straws are the equivalent of a buttery, savory cookie. They are a highly addictive and popular holiday snack often gifted and quickly devoured. I've never eaten a version I didn't like, but the spicy ones rank at the top of my list. They come in a variety of shapes, though I have always found this French fry interpretation to be the most fun. Enjoy them as a morning treat or afternoon snack: Dip them in a sunny-side-up egg or in a hot bowl of tomato soup.

Preheat the oven to 350°F (180°C). Line a rimmed large baking sheet with a silicone baking mat or a layer of parchment paper.

In a medium bowl, whisk together the flour, salt, red pepper flakes, paprika, cayenne pepper, and onion powder. Set the flour mixture aside.

Place the butter and Cheddar cheese in the bowl of a stand mixer fitted with a paddle attachment. Beat the butter and Cheddar cheese together at medium speed until they are just combined. Add the milk and continue mixing the ingredients at medium speed while spooning in the flour mixture. Mix the ingredients for 1 to 2 minutes, until all the ingredients are incorporated and a dough forms.

Lightly dust a work surface with flour, then dust a rolling pin with flour. Remove the dough from the stand mixer's bowl and place it on the prepared work surface. Roll out the dough until it is ¼ inch (6 mm) thick.

Using a fluted pastry cutting wheel, cut the dough into strips that are 2 inches (5 cm) long and ½ inch (1.3 cm) wide. Transfer the strips to the prepared baking sheet, spacing them 1 inch (2.5 cm) apart.

Bake the cheese straws on the oven's middle rack for 12 to 14 minutes, or until they are light brown on the bottoms and edges. Remove the baking sheet from the oven and set it on a wire rack for 20 minutes. Transfer the cheese straws to the wire rack to completely cool. Finally, transfer the cheese straws to clear Mason jars or gift bags for gifting.

BREAKFAST "QUICHE" PIE

YIELDS

8 servings

SWEET POTATO CRUST

2 sweet potatoes, peeled

1 tbsp (8 g) all-purpose flour

½ tsp sea salt

½ tsp freshly ground black pepper

½ tsp paprika

¼ tsp onion powder

1½ tbsp (21 g) unsalted butter, melted and cooled

1 large egg, lightly beaten

FILLING

8 oz (224 g) ground spicy pork sausage

3 tbsp (42 g) unsalted butter

1 yellow onion, diced

1 cup (100 g) finely chopped mixed mushrooms (see Note)

2 cups (60 g) baby spinach, roughly chopped

8 large eggs

1½ cups (360 ml) heavy cream

½ tsp sea salt

½ tsp freshly ground black pepper

1 tsp minced fresh sage

2 cups (126 g) grated Gruyère cheese, divided

Let's talk about quiche, or what I like to call breakfast pie! It is a mixture of meat, cheeses, and veggies that makes me completely forget about omelets. Quiche can be made with the Herb and Cheese Galette Crust on page 12, or try this fun sweet potato crust. I prefer to bake quiche in a cast-iron skillet, like the familiar sausage and egg casserole served at family breakfasts. This quiche will keep you fully satisfied until lunch!

Start by preheating the oven to 425°F (220°C). Set out a cast-iron skillet that is 9 inches (23 cm) in diameter and 2 inches (5 cm) deep.

Prepare the sweet potato crust by shredding the sweet potatoes—you should end up with about 3 cups (300 g). Place the shredded sweet potatoes on a layer of paper towels and squeeze them in the paper towels to soak up any extra moisture. Transfer the sweet potatoes to a medium bowl. Add the flour, salt, black pepper, paprika, onion powder, butter, and egg and stir with a rubber spatula to evenly distribute them throughout the sweet potatoes. Dump the sweet potato mixture into the cast-iron skillet. Use your fingers to press the mixture evenly into the bottom and up the sides of the skillet to create a bottom crust.

Loosely cover the skillet with aluminum foil. Bake the crust on the oven's middle rack for 25 minutes. Remove the skillet from the oven and place the skillet on a wire rack until you are ready to add the filling.

Reduce the oven's temperature to 375°F (190°C).

Make the filling. Cook the sausage in a medium skillet over medium-high heat for 4 to 6 minutes, until the sausage is cooked through and crumbled. Transfer the sausage to a plate lined with paper towels to absorb excess grease. Set the plate aside.

Wipe the skillet clean and set it over low heat. Add the butter and onion. Cook the onion for 20 minutes, stirring it every 2 minutes. The onion should be caramelized and a nice golden brown. Transfer the onion to a small bowl and set it aside.

Return the skillet to low heat. Add the mushrooms to the skillet and cook them for 3 to 4 minutes, until they have browned and softened. Transfer the mushrooms to the bowl of onion. Place the spinach in the skillet and cook it for about 30 seconds, until it is slightly wilted, then transfer the spinach to the bowl of onion and mushrooms.

(CONTINUED)

BREAKFAST "QUICHE" PIE (CONTINUED)

In a large bowl, stir together the eggs, heavy cream, salt, black pepper, and sage. Add the sausage, onion, mushrooms, spinach, and 1½ cups (94 g) of the Gruyère cheese and stir the ingredients until everything is evenly distributed. Transfer the filling to the partially baked crust, and then sprinkle the remaining ½ cup (32 g) of Gruyère cheese on top.

Cover the skillet with a loosely tented piece of aluminum foil. Place the skillet on the oven's middle rack. Bake the quiche for 40 minutes, then remove the aluminum foil and bake the quiche for 10 minutes. The center of the quiche should be almost set. If it's a little soft, that's fine; just make sure it's not jiggling.

Remove the skillet from the oven. Place the skillet on a wire rack to cool for 10 minutes, then slice the quiche and serve it warm.

NOTE

I recommend a mixture of cremini and chanterelle mushrooms for this dish.

Acknowledgments

Who would have thought a horse-crazy girl with a love for photography would evolve into a passionate baker? The route from animal science to playing with pie dough may seem like a rather circuitous path, but I will be forever grateful for the wild ride that has brought me to this point in my life.

With this cookbook, I am sending out a huge thank-you to all the readers of my little baking blog, Two Cups Flour. I shared my first recipe post with you in the spring of 2018, and I have been covered in flour ever since. Testing recipes and sharing my love for fun food with you is what I live for now. And when you proudly show your baked goods to me, it warms my heart. I appreciate you all so very, very much.

Mom and Dad, you instilled in me a love and appreciation for food, hard work, and following my passions. I'm so grateful to have you as inspiration, taste testers, and my cheer squad. I will never be able to thank you enough for supporting me every step of the way. I love you both so much!

My dear and wonderful friends, thank you for understanding when I needed to lock myself in the kitchen for months. Thank you for lending me your ears as I discussed flavor combinations and food-styling ideas. I cherish you all and cannot wait to spend time together eating delicious food.

Thank you to my lovely neighbors for accepting my constant food drop-offs and requests for feedback. I could not ask for better recipe reviewers—you always keep it real.

To my editor, Marissa: I'm so thankful for your help with this exciting process. I would have never been able to organize this book without you. You kept me going when I needed it most.

About the Author

Jenn Davis is a true southern girl, born, raised, and spending most of her life in North Carolina, a few years in Nashville, and now residing in Louisville, Kentucky. She started baking with her mother as a young child, fell in love with art, and has spent the years since combining these two passions through recipes and food photography. After posting her first blog recipe to Two Cups Flour in the spring of 2018, Jenn became obsessed with flavor combinations, food styling, and capturing her creations in a whimsical, vintage style of photography. Two Cups Flour was a *Saveur* Best Baking Blog finalist for 2018 and the winner for Best Blog Photography in 2019. Jenn works as a freelance recipe developer, food stylist, and food photographer. She spends her free time gardening, traveling, and playing with her dog, Mojito.

Index